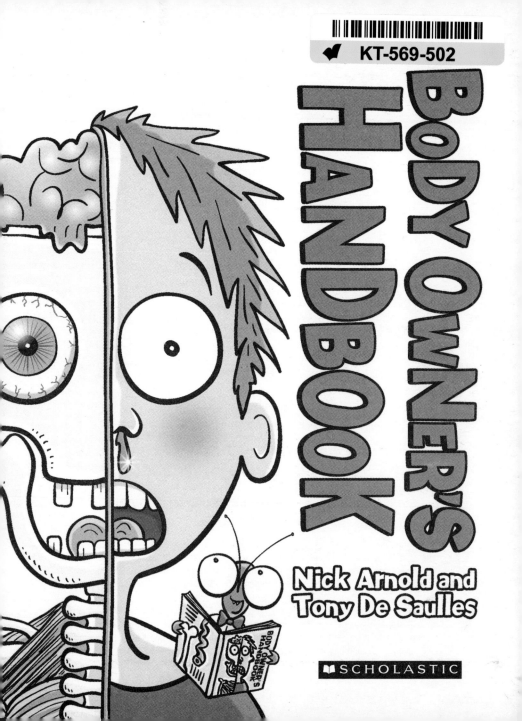

BODY OWNER'S HANDBOOK

Nick Arnold and Tony De Saulles

SCHOLASTIC

www.scholastic.co.uk

Scholastic Children's Books,
Euston House, 24 Eversholt Street,
London NW1 1DB, UK

A division of Scholastic Ltd
London ~ New York ~ Toronto ~ Sydney ~ Auckland
Mexico City ~ New Delhi ~ Hong Kong

First published in the UK by Scholastic Ltd, 2002
This revised and updated edition published by Scholastic Ltd, 2014

ISBN 978 1407 14450 4

Printed and bound by CPI Group (UK) Ltd, Croydon, CR0 4YY

2 4 6 8 10 9 7 5 3

CONTENTS

Nick Arnold has been writing stories and books since he was a youngster, but never dreamt he'd find fame writing a handbook for body owners. His research involved getting to grips with preserved body bits, studying snot and examining ear wax and he enjoyed every minute of it.

When he's not delving into Horrible Science, he spends his spare time eating pizza, riding his bike and thinking up corny jokes (though not all at the same time).

www.nickarnold-website.com

Tony De Saulles picked up his crayons when he was still in nappies and has been doodling ever since. He takes Horrible Science very seriously and even agreed to test cures for baldness. Fortunately, he's made a full recovery. When he's not out with his sketchpad, Tony likes to write poetry and play squash, though he hasn't written any poetry about squash yet.

www.tonydesaulles.co.uk

INTRODUCTION

You and I and everyone on Planet Earth have something in common. Each of us owns an incredible walking, talking machine. You can even spend your whole life living inside it. I'm talking about your very own human body! Yes – each one of us is a *human body owner*! And that's where our problems begin...

You see, the human body needs lots of looking after, but there's no user guide to show us what to do! No wonder body problems cause such grief! Wouldn't it be *brilliant* if there was a helpful handbook with advice on basic body repairs and avoiding body breakdowns?

Well, now there is! And guess what? You're actually reading it! So, WELCOME TO THE WORLD'S FIRST BODY OWNER'S HANDBOOK!

Of course, there are lots of different human bodies. Just walk down the road and you're sure to see many bodies in all shapes and sizes, ages and states of repair...

SPOTTERS' GUIDE TO BODY TYPES

SHUFFLE! TODDLE! AMBLE! WEE! STROLL! STRIDE! SKATE! CHAT! WOBBLE!

OLD WOMAN

DAD WITH TODDLER

YOUNG WOMAN

TEENAGER

YOUNG BOY

MOTHER AND BABY

YOUNG GIRL | MIDDLE-AGED MAN | OLD MAN | MIDDLE-AGED WOMAN | YOUNG MAN

But this handbook is designed for every body around today – and that includes *your* body!

So read on and find out how to get the very best from your body. Check out what's right for it, and what isn't. See what each body bit does and how to tackle body breakdown problems. Find out everything you wanted to know about your body and never dared to ask – and more!

But be warned – some body facts can be shocking. And this handbook won't hold back from telling you like it is. After all it's your body, and you've got every right to know what's going on inside it...

BODY BITS FOR BEGINNERS

In a moment we'll open up the body to find out how it works. But first an important message …

CONGRATULATIONS ON OWNING THE BEST BODY MACHINE IN THE UNIVERSE! It really is: for once the adverts are spot-on…

LOOKING FOR A NEW BODY?

WHY NOT CHOOSE THE REAL MCCOY - THE ONE AND ONLY
HUMAN BODY

IT'S PLANET EARTH'S MOST ADVANCED LIVING MACHINE! It's built of the finest materials to a tried and tested design that's over *two hundred thousand* years old! With a bit of care and attention your human body will provide over EIGHTY YEARS of superb service!

IT'S TRUE!

OLD MAN

During this time your top-of-the-range human body is designed to...

▶ Talk for ten years. YAK! YAK!

▶ Eat for 3.5 years. MUNCH!

▶ Take MILLIONS of steps and cover 22,500 km (14,000 miles). (The body can walk 19,000 steps every day without its feet falling off.) WALK!

FLEX!

▶ Bend and straighten its fingers 25 million times without needing new knuckles.

PUMP!

▶ Beat its heart blood-pump over 2.5 billion times non-stop at an average 73 beats a minute, 105,120 beats a day. (Every 24 hours the heart pumps 8 to 16,000 litres of blood and never goes pop!)

THINK! ▷ store ONE MILLION bits of data in its brain memory - everything from science facts to shopping lists, plus your friends' birthdays, 100,000 words, all the players in your favourite team - and it can recognize over 2,000 faces!

~THE SMALL PRINT~
Remember, the body is designed to do these things over its lifetime. Body owners shouldn't expect their bodies to do them all non-stop!

The human body comes in two main body models - the MALE and the FEMALE, and both body models are available in a lovely choice of colours!

available in: light brown, dark brown, pink, beige and yellow

WOMAN
GIRL
BOY
MAN

THE HUMAN BODY - BET YOU CAN'T LIVE WITHOUT IT!

This handbook contains important warnings for body owners – please read them carefully. Here's the first:

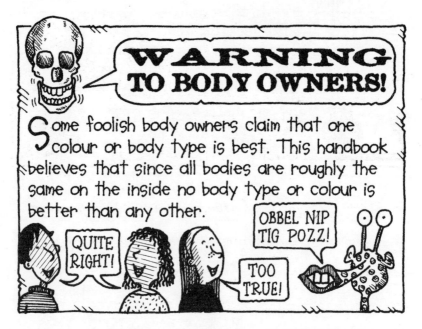

The body sounds pretty impressive, eh? And did you spot the best-selling point of all? The human body has been designed to carry on working for over *80 years* – and some bodies are still going strong after 120 years! And that's *loads* longer than most animal bodies…

- Sparrows hop the twig after 18 months.

- Dormice are dead as doornails after five years.
- Swans sing their swan-songs after seven years.
- Dogs bow-wow out after ten years.
- Cats come a cropper after 15 years.

But body owners may be disappointed to learn that their human body won't last as long as some animal bodies…

• The oldest tortoise plodded on for 150 years.

• Sharks and lobsters seem to go on and on without showing signs of age until they're finished off by other animals.

AND I'LL FINISH OFF WITH THE SHARK-FIN SOUP

Mind you, 99.9% of human body owners wouldn't swap their bodies for anything else. I mean, who'd want a body that lumbers around eating lettuce all day?

Well, now you've found out how amazing your body is, I bet you're itching to take a peep at the working bits inside. Don't worry, this is quite normal. *But DON'T do it!* The body isn't designed to be opened by non-experts and this can result in serious body breakdowns!

For example, in 1994 a French postman cut open his own body to check that surgeons had removed a body bit called the appendix. His body suffered a total body breakdown — this is also known as death. What that postie needed was a body-bit checklist with details of what each body part is designed to do. Then he might have found out what was going on inside his body without looking inside. Well, as luck would have it, this handbook features just such a checklist and it's coming up next…

THE BODY-BIT CHECKLIST

All the body bits pictured below were supplied by our scientific expert, the one and only madly famous, famously mad scientist – Baron Frankenstein. It seems the Baron has quite a collection…

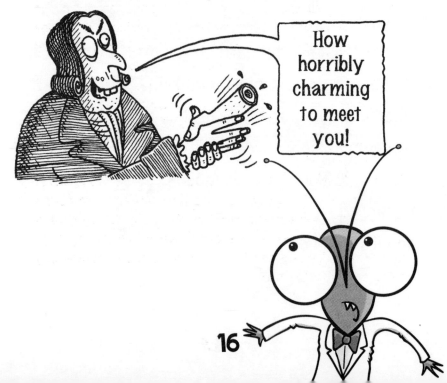

☑ The incredible stretchy body covering

The first thing you notice when you look at your body is the super-stretchy outer-body cover (also known as the skin). Your skin is a self-cooling germ-proof wrap-around coating designed to protect your delicate body bits.

COLOUR: PALE BROWN

SIZE: 9-10 YEARS

HUMAN SKIN TO FIT SKELETON OF BOY

Your skin is programmed to replace itself when it's worn out and it even repairs itself when damaged. But it's got one annoying design defect. Worn-out skin flakes off over the carpet. During its lifetime the human body sheds 47.6 kg of waste skin. That's equal to *one thousand* layers of skin or *five* bulging rubbish sacks!

Your skin is only 0.5 mm thick, but it's surprisingly big and baggy. If you stripped the skin off a large male body and rolled it flat (a messy job, so you'd best not try it!) the skin would cover up to two square metres. This skin weighs about the same as three winter overcoats.

If you look closely at your body you might spot a few moles. NO, not those funny underground animals that eat worms! Body moles are brown blobs of a substance called melanin. Melanin is your skin's fully automatic self-darkening sun-defence system. It's designed to darken to protect your body against sunburn. The skin markings known as freckles are also blobs of melanin and that's why they become darker in the sun.

☑ The multi-stranded head cover

Next it's time to check the multi-stranded thermal head-covering feature known to body owners as hair. This body part is made up of about 100,000 hairs (older bodies may have less – see page 176 for the bald facts).

Each hair is squeezed from a tiny pit on your head at a speed of 1 cm per month. In a year, your body makes 12 km of the stuff – about 1,000 km in an average body lifetime or enough hair to stretch from London to Paris by road and back again. If your hair wasn't cut and didn't fall out, you would grow hair, there and everywhere...

☑ Water-deflectors

These strange hairy caterpillar-like objects, commonly known as eyebrows, are designed to stop sweat from your body's automatic water-cooling system trickling down into your eyes.

You'll be shocked to know, dear reader, that your human body has more hairs than a chimpanzee! The only reason your body doesn't look like King Kong is because its hairs are finer and shorter and harder to see.

BODY LANGUAGE

Body owners may find it useful to understand the jargon used by experts. Don't worry, this handbook will supply you with enough word power to stagger a body expert (also known as a scientist).

How would you feel if your body has rutilism?

ANSWER

Quite right! Rutilism is the body expert's word for *red hair*. Red hair contains iron and the red colour is caused by a rusting effect! Other hair colours are caused by the amount of melanin they contain, but auburn hair is a mix of red hair and melanin. By the way, body owners, red hair might be "rusty" but it doesn't squeak – so put that oil can down!

☑ Built-in finger and toe protectors

Your body is equipped with tough finger and toe protectors called nails. Your body has been programmed to automatically replace its nails over time. Every day the fingernails get longer by the width of two hairs and if you didn't cut these nails your body would produce 28 metres of nails during its life-time!

NOSE PICKING IS A BIT TRICKY THESE DAYS

Younger bodies produce nails faster than older bodies – especially if the nails are nibbled. Tut tut!

☑ The central information-processing unit

Your body's top-of-the-range highly advanced information-processing unit is known as the brain. In order to function properly your brain needs to be kept warmer than the rest of your body. It also consumes up to 20% of your body's fuel (known as food) – that's more than any other body part. Your brain also needs 16 times more oxygen (the gas your body takes from the air) than any other body bit.

As a body owner you don't need to know the details of how your brain works (scientists are still puzzling over some of these), but it helps to have some idea of what's going on in there. Baron Frankenstein has kindly chopped a spare brain in half so we can see the main bits. Thanks, Baron!

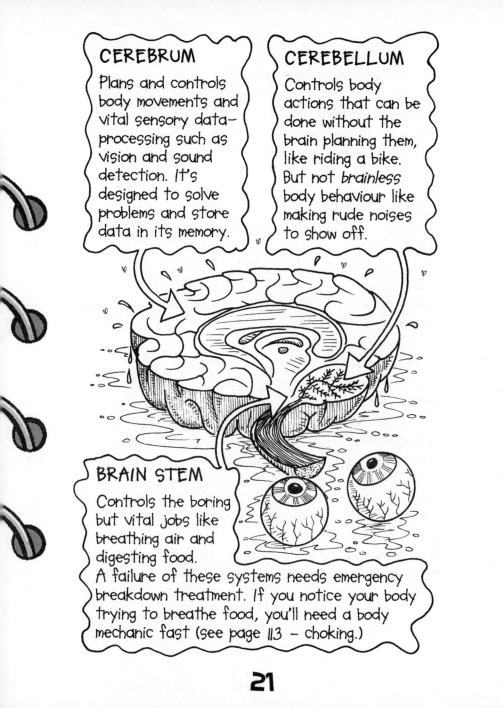

CEREBRUM

Plans and controls body movements and vital sensory data-processing such as vision and sound detection. It's designed to solve problems and store data in its memory.

CEREBELLUM

Controls body actions that can be done without the brain planning them, like riding a bike. But not *brainless* body behaviour like making rude noises to show off.

BRAIN STEM

Controls the boring but vital jobs like breathing air and digesting food.

A failure of these systems needs emergency breakdown treatment. If you notice your body trying to breathe food, you'll need a body mechanic fast (see page 113 — choking.)

21

Every day your body automatically produces half a glass of brain juice for your brain to float around in. This watery stuff cushions your brain inside its protection shield (or skull, as it's called). And every day some brain juice oozes back into the blood — you might call this a fluid situation, ha ha!

BODY LANGUAGE

A body expert says...

YOU'VE GOT A BLUE SPOT...

Do you say...

NO, THEY'RE RED WITH WHITE BITS IN THE MIDDLE!

No, your body really does have a blue spot … *in your brain!* The blue spot pumps out a chemical that powers up your brain when anything interesting grabs its attention. Stuff like learning a really cool fact or spotting a hungry-looking dinosaur. So now for some interesting info to get that blue spot squirting…

BODY DATA

Your brain uses **LESS** energy watching TV than doing nothing! No wonder watching the shopping channel can send your brain into shutdown mode – otherwise known as sleep. It can even result in digestive juice leaking from your food entry hatch (this is also known as dribbling).

You can train your brain to get better at a task by practising. For example, practising a musical instrument improves control of the movements needed. It also develops the area of your brain that deals with music. This is how I learnt to play the church organ madly at the dead of night — ha ha!

☑ The fully automated blood pump and air inlet/exhaust system

Along with your brain, the fully automated long-life blood pump, or heart, is your body's most vital part. It's basically a non-stop fluid-flow control booster. It's powerful enough to pump all your blood around your body in one minute. If need be it can do this heart-thumping job in just ten seconds!

Listen well, dear reader: the bigger the body, the slower the heartbeat. An elephant heart beats more slowly than the human heart, which beats more slowly than a cat heart. Indeed, I should know — I've cut out a good many hearts in my time!

Lungs are your body's self-regulating air inlet and exhaust system. They take oxygen from the air into your blood and puff out carbon-dioxide gas. (You can find out why this is important on page 114.)

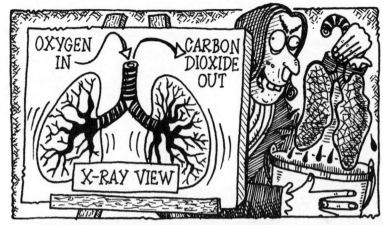

OXYGEN IN → CARBON DIOXIDE OUT

X-RAY VIEW

☑ The internal fluid transportation system

Your body comes equipped with a state-of-the-art fluid transport system. And although it looks like a gloopy red liquid, your body's five litres (8.8 pints) of blood are swarming with tiny red and white blood cells! Each of these units functions like a micro-engineered robot with a job to do inside the body. Red blood cells carry oxygen through the blood tubes known as blood vessels and white blood cells fight germs.

BODY DATA

Unlike other machines, your body machine may be attacked by microbes. Harmful microbes are known as germs and they can multiply inside the body and destroy its cells. This is a major body design problem, but you'll be relieved to know that your body has been programmed to defend itself (see page 138 for the details).

25

Blood also carries food to your body bits. Your body has 96,000 km of blood vessels. (You may wonder how they all fit in – it's bleeding amazing!)

RED BLOOD CELLS

According to my dear un-dead friend Count Dracula, red blood cells are bright red when they carry oxygen and dark red without it. Under pale skin dark red blood shows up as a tasteful shade of blue. The Count says that bright red blood tastes best. I find the Count good company although some people think he's a pain in the neck, ha ha!

☑ The fuel storage tank and conveyor belt

This system (often known as the stomach and guts) breaks down food and fuels your body. Body experts call this process digestion and describe the stomach and guts as the digestive system. Every day your guts process ten litres of sloppy, half-digested food. And this fully automated 24-hour operation also handles liquid fuels (known as drinks).

The system works by pumping out chemically engineered digestive juices such as spit that help to break food chemicals up. The juices are made in special production units called glands and squirted out automatically. Spit, for example, squirts into your mouth whenever your body's sensory system detects food.

Your body's fully automated guts are designed to shift half-digested food by about 2.8 cm per minute. And unused food is ejected from your rear-end gas vent/solid-waste ejection pipe after about 24 hours.

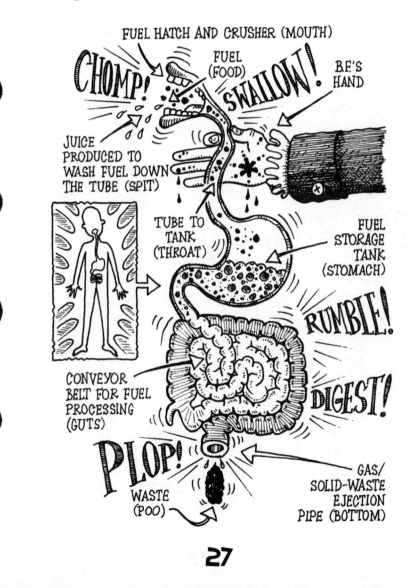

FUEL HATCH AND CRUSHER (MOUTH)

CHOMP!

FUEL (FOOD)

SWALLOW!

BF'S HAND

JUICE PRODUCED TO WASH FUEL DOWN THE TUBE (SPIT)

TUBE TO TANK (THROAT)

FUEL STORAGE TANK (STOMACH)

RUMBLE!

CONVEYOR BELT FOR FUEL PROCESSING (GUTS)

DIGEST!

PLOP!

WASTE (POO)

GAS/ SOLID-WASTE EJECTION PIPE (BOTTOM)

☑ The multi-functional food and chemical processor

The liver is your body's fully portable multi-functional chemical processing unit. It weighs 1.5 kg – slightly heavier than your brain, but like your brain it's designed to fit inside your body and be carried about. Your liver is a precisely engineered system designed to sort out and store the vital food substances – sugars, proteins, fats. What's more, it's equipped with an amazing automatic rebuild feature that allows it to re-form after damage. In fact, your liver can replace itself from just a sliver of liver!

☑ Heavy-duty fluid filters

Your body automatically cleans and controls the amount of water in your blood using a pair of heavy-duty fluid filters known as kidneys. Your kidneys remove waste chemicals and spare water from the blood. The waste then goes on a one-way trip to the toilet (via the liquid waste store or bladder, and the liquid waste outflow pipe).

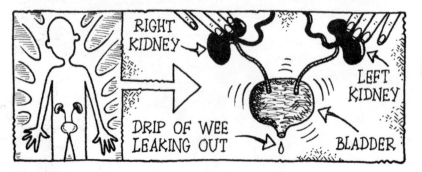

Every day your kidneys check every drop of blood 36 times and produce 1.5 litres of yellow body waste or pee as it's often called. Over the course of its lifetime your body can produce about 40,000 litres of pee – that's enough to fill four road tankers!

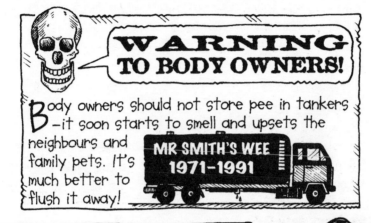

WARNING TO BODY OWNERS!

Body owners should not store pee in tankers – it soon starts to smell and upsets the neighbours and family pets. It's much better to flush it away!

MR SMITH'S WEE 1971–1991

Well, the author may think that urine (the proper name for liquid waste) should be flushed away. But I think it's an excellent gargle and mouthwash! I'll tell you more on page 142. Cheers!

BODY DATA

One really revolting pee ingredient is called urea. This chemical contains poisonous ammonia from waste protein. If it builds up it can cause a total body breakdown. That's why your body is so desperate to get rid of it. Urea also turns up in skin, and hair and nails. Yes, it's in fingernails – now that really is something to chew over!

☑ Building blocks for body bits

At this point all you body owners out there may be wondering what kind of substance your body's skin and brain and kidneys and body bits are actually *made of*. Well, rather confusingly, your body isn't supplied with a list of ingredients. In fact, it has no labelling of any kind, not even a bar code on its bum...

Anyway, the thing you need to know is that the main material of your body is plain simple good-old-fashioned WATER. Take away water and your body would be a powdery mass weighing just 40% of its original body weight. The powder includes substances that make up the bones (see page 33) and other vital chemicals.

Most of your body's complicated chemicals are arranged in tiny self-contained self-replacing micro-engineered units known as cells. Do you remember the red and white blood cells on page 25? In fact, your body has 100,000,000,000,000 (one hundred thousand billion) cells, er – give or take a few billion.

Hey, body owners – stop right there! Let's take a deep breath and *think* about that number. Even *one million* is a horribly huge figure. In 1982, Australian Les Stewart decided to type every number from one to one million (don't ask me why). It took him *sixteen years* and

19,990 sheets of paper. But at that rate it would take Les over *one hundred million years* to number the cells in his own body! And by then he'd have run out of fingers to count with.

TEN MILLION AND THREE...

A cell is too tiny to see without a microscope and yet it's as complex as a small city. But amazingly your body automatically produces *one billion cells* every hour. Younger bodies are programmed to grow larger by making lots of extra cells, but all human bodies replace cells that break down. In just one day your body makes more cells than there are human bodies on Earth! No wonder smaller bodies get worn out at school!

The cell replacement programme is vital to keep your body on the road. Here's a typical body cell breakdown-and-replacement job sheet...

THE BODY REPAIR SHOP

CELL-REPLACEMENT SCHEDULE

Check when cells need replacing. Fit new ones as and when the old ones break down...

* Red blood cells should keep going for six months without too much bother.

* Liver cells "liver" for five months, ha ha! Just keep an eye on them...

* Skin cells last three to four weeks – replace them to keep bodywork in good condition.

* Stomach, gut and mouth cells last for just three days – these will need constant work, tut tut!

* Check cells that produce new bone – they're supposed to make a new skeleton body frame every seven years to replace lost bone cells.

IF WE DON'T DO THESE JOBS IT COSTS THE BODY OWNER AN ARM AND A LEG! MIND YOU WE CAN'T REPLACE LOST TEETH OR KIDNEY TUBES OR MOST BRAIN CELLS, AND WE CAN'T PUT NEW EGGS INTO A FEMALE BODY (SEE PAGE 186). NONE OF THESE ARE DESIGNED TO BE REPLACED. YOU JUST CAN'T GET THE PARTS, GUV.

So prepare yourself for a shock. That means… Most of your body bits are less than *ten years old*! Even battered old bodies are mostly *no older* than a good-condition ten-year-old body! You can find out why older bodies look so ancient on page 172, but right now we've got to finish off the checklist…

☑ Body framework and motors

Your body's super-strong support framework (often called the skeleton) is designed to stop it flopping all over the floor. It's actually made of 206 interconnected units called bones made of a unique high-endurance mixture of calcium and phosphate chemicals with added protein called collagen. Your skeleton weighs 9 kg and it's been engineered to carry five times its own weight without breaking.

Your bones are usually connected by shock-absorbers called joints. The joint shock-absorbers protect your body by cushioning the bones in bags of squishy fluid. The ends of your bones are coated in a soft shock-proof substance called cartilage. This protection is vital because the joints take a lot of wear and tear – an ankle joint bears the force of ten times your body's weight every time it hops. Yet the joint is strong enough to help your body take millions of steps without squeaking or going rusty.

BODY DATA

1 When your body does a sit-up exercise, your lower backbone carries the same weight as 174 metres of water crushing a diver.

2 When your body lands after a high jump, your bones take the force of nine tonnes. That's the weight of three cars or one and a half elephants. (Body owners should never try to lift even half an elephant. This may result in severe body damage and getting covered in elephant poo!)

One of the most vital parts of your skeleton is the vertical support column (also known as the backbone or spine). It's actually 33 bony plates arranged in a springy S-shaped curve. This soaks up some of the force of walking, but strains (see page 88) cause back damage in some bodies.

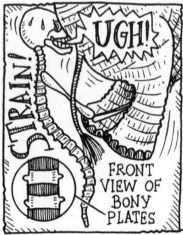

STRAIN!

UGH!

FRONT VIEW OF BONY PLATES

BODY DATA

1 Does your body ever make strange noises? I'm sure you've heard cracking sounds when fingers are straightened or creaking knees and clicking ankle joints. These odd sounds are perfectly normal – and believe it or not they're made by bubbles. Normally, bubbles of nitrogen gas are dissolved in the liquid that cushions the joints. They're like bubbles in fizzy lemonade before you open it.

2 When the joint is forced apart, bubbles appear as the pressure is released, just like when you open that lemonade. The bubbles pop and you hear a cracking noise. Fortunately these noisy joints don't start burping afterwards.

☑ High-performance motor power units

Your body's power-unit motors are known as muscles. Every body is equipped with more than 600 muscles. They're controlled by nerve signals from your brain and pull on your bones with extra-tough cables called tendons. (Nerves are your body's high-tech telephone wires for messages to and from the brain.)

TEST YOUR BODY 1:
JUST NOSING AROUND

Is your body up to its design standard? This handbook offers you, the body owner, a chance to find out with the aid of a unique series of body tests. Here's test number one.

You will need:

A MONSTER (IF YOU HAVEN'T GOT ONE, USE YOUR OWN BODY)

A MIRROR

What you do:
1 Get your body to wrinkle its nose, like so...

WRINKLE! EASY!

2 Now try to do it without moving
its upper lip...

You should find:
It's impossible for the body to
wrinkle its nose without lifting its
upper lip. This is because the same
muscle controls both movements.

What an uplifting test! But then your body's muscle engineering is incredibly impressive — yes it is, body owners — even if your body is fitted with low-power mini-muscles.

But I'm sorry to say that your human body doesn't measure up too well against some animal bodies. Few human bodies have ever managed to move at more than 43.5 km (27 miles) per hour – and only for a few seconds. But that's just a gentle jog for some creatures. Cheetahs chase about at 101 km (62.75 miles) per hour – and if an ant grew as big as your body, it would power through your picnic at 150 km (93 miles) per hour! Ant that amazin', body owners?

A MESSAGE TO BODY OWNERS...

Not every body can reach the body's top speed, but if your body is more of a tired tortoise than a charging cheetah, don't despair! Your body is still a high-tech machine with awesome automatic features that would turn a robot green with envy. Well, that's if robots *could* turn green! Anyway, you'd best read on and check if your body's auto-systems are working...

AUTOMATIC BODY FEATURES

Your body has been designed to suck in air, sense its surroundings and protect itself from dirt and dust. And the really amazing thing about these features is that they're *fully automatic*. So that means you, the body owner, don't have to switch them on in the morning. Let's begin with…

THE AUTOMATIC AIR INLET/ EXHAUST SYSTEM

A vital automatic function (known as breathing) supplies your body with oxygen from the air. Without it your body would suffer total breakdown in *three minutes*. But since the breathing function is always switched on, you can relax and forget about it.

Mind you, the breathing function is so amazingly designed that body experts get quite breathless about it! What happens is a sheet of muscle under the lungs called the diaphragm (dia-fram) pulls down whilst your rib cage pulls up and out ...

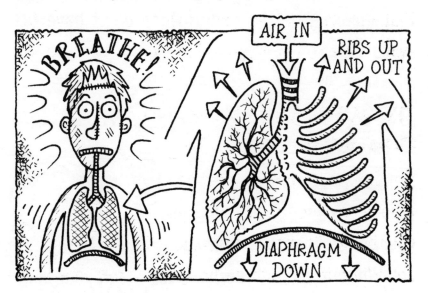

Air rushes down your gas feeder tube (known as the windpipe) into the lungs. When your body isn't active, the best way for it to breathe is through the airborne chemical sampling chamber (or nose space) – the entrance nozzles are often known as nostrils.

NOSE BREATHING PROCEDURE

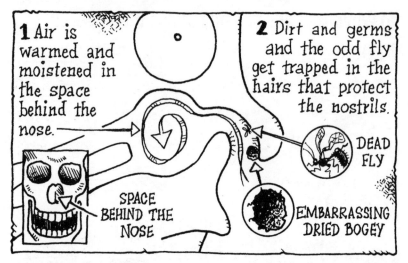

1 Air is warmed and moistened in the space behind the nose.

SPACE BEHIND THE NOSE

2 Dirt and germs and the odd fly get trapped in the hairs that protect the nostrils.

DEAD FLY

EMBARRASSING DRIED BOGEY

Oddly enough, your body doesn't use 30% of its breathed-in air. In order to breathe out, your body automatically relaxes the diaphragm muscle and lowers the rib cage – forcing air from your lungs. In 21 years, your body puffs out enough air to fill 3.5 million balloons. This could be useful if you're planning to treat your body to a big 21st Birthday Bash.

Sometimes your body breathes in an odd fashion known as yawning. Your body yawns:

a) When it is need of shut-down mode (sleep).

b) During boring science lessons.

No one knows why bodies yawn, but it could be some sort of signal because when one body yawns others often join in. Does looking at this picture make your body yawn…?

I said … oh no, I told you it was catching!

KEEPING THE VITAL TUBES CLEAR

Sometimes debris such as dust, germs and bits of fly avoid your nostril hairs and get breathed in by accident. Fortunately your body has another automatic procedure to deal with the problem. In this handbook it's known as the AWESOMELY INCREDIBLE SNOT CONVEYOR BELT. Here's how it works…

AWESOMELY INCREDIBLE SNOT CONVEYOR BELT

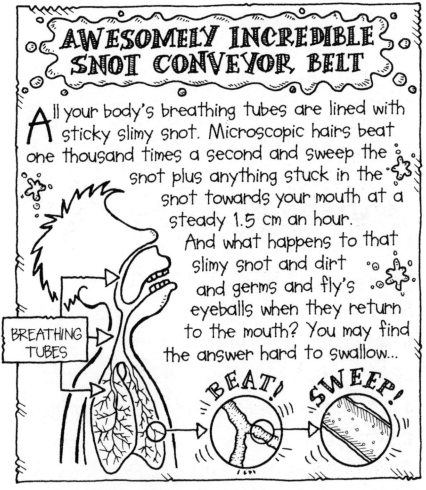

All your body's breathing tubes are lined with sticky slimy snot. Microscopic hairs beat one thousand times a second and sweep the snot plus anything stuck in the snot towards your mouth at a steady 1.5 cm an hour.

And what happens to that slimy snot and dirt and germs and fly's eyeballs when they return to the mouth? You may find the answer hard to swallow...

BREATHING TUBES

BEAT!

SWEEP!

And now for the first in our exclusive series of real-life stories that show the body in action.

Curious case study: Dangerous dribbling

Your body is designed to spit gooey drool globs but this isn't the sort of skill you want to show off in public. Not only is it gross – it can cause accidents. In 1977 French body owner Claude Antoine was spitting whilst hurling his body across an upstairs room. Guess what happened when he got to an open window? Claude's battered body required a long stay in a body repair facility (otherwise known as a hospital).

BODY LANGUAGE

A body expert announces:

No. Mucus is the body expert's name for snot – and it's also found in spit.

If anything bigger than a microbe gets into your body's breathing tubes, your body activates its automatic particle ejection programme – this is known as sneezing or coughing. Sneezing gets rid of anything that upsets the sensitive upper throat area such as dust.

And coughing splutters out any nasty stuff that falls further down the windpipe.

BODY DATA

1 In 1635, Dr William Lee announced that the human body sneezes when the sun's heat draws moisture from the brain into the nose. Modern body experts are quite sniffy about this idea.

2 The World Sneezing Record is held by a 12-year-old British girl who sneezed for **TWO AND HALF YEARS** from 1981 to 1983. She atishoo'ed **ONE MILLION** times a year – an achievement not to be sniffed at.

3 During a sneeze your eyelids close automatically to stop blood vessels breaking and making your eyes look bloodshot. Even if your eyes stay open – they **WON'T** plop from their sockets because strong muscles hold them in position.

And whilst we're talking about eyes, let's spot another range of automatic body features: the sensory data-collection systems – including, of course, the visual-input system…

AUTOMATIC SENSORY EQUIPMENT

Your body receives visual data through two high-tech light receptors known as eyeballs. This process is known as seeing. Each eyeball weighs seven grams and is designed to sense light falling on millions of light-sensitive cells in the retina area at the back of each eyeball. The retina fires data to your brain via a high-speed cable of two million nerve fibres.

AUTOMATIC EYE-WASHING FEATURE

Your eyeballs have a unique automatic self-cleaning feature that means you never have to stop to clean your eyeballs. Instead each eyeball has a protective loose skin-cover or eyelid. Your eyelids close automatically – it's called blinking – and each time this happens they wash your eyeballs with a cleaning fluid known as tears.

Actually, your body produces different types of tears that form protective layers over your eyeballs. There's a layer of gooey snotty tears (with mucus) on the eyeball's surface. Above this you'll find ordinary tears, and on top are oily tears that stop the other tears drying up. Yes, tears are so good it would be a crying shame if you ever ran out of them!

Your eyes blink between ten and 24 times a minute – that's millions of times a year. According to body experts if your body gets damaged, your eyes blink more often. But if your body is just ticking over or reading, it blinks less, as these photos of the Monster prove…

ARRRRRRRRRGH!

BLINK! BLINK! BLINK!

MONSTER SITTING ON A DRAWING PIN...

HMM, GREAT BOOK!

BLINK!

MONSTER READING A HORRIBLE SCIENCE BOOK...

Tear production units over your nose pump out the cleaning fluid. Sometimes large amounts of tears are produced – this procedure is known as crying. As a result the nose can become embarrassingly snotty and needs to be blown gently (see page 74). Then, during the night, the tears dry to sleepy dust. Aaah!

BODY DATA

1 Crying takes place when your brain processor runs complex data programmes known as feelings. These might be happy or sad or angry or mixed-up feelings or wanting attention signals. No wonder some body owners feel totally confused about feelings.

2 Elephants have drippy eyes and crocodiles make tears to get rid of salt (I guess they're only crocodile tears) – but they can't compete with the blubbering body. In its wimpy-weepy lifetime the human body squirts out 85 litres of tears – that's about 1,850,000 teardrops and quite few soggy hankies.

HIGH-TECH TOUCH-SENSOR SYSTEMS

Your body's skin is supplied with millions of inbuilt high-tech micro-sensor units. Some are designed to detect pressure and others are sensitive to temperature changes or lighter touch, and all are linked via nerves to the brain. Here's your chance to test them...

TEST YOUR BODY 2: A TOUCHING MOMENT
You will need:
• Your body
• A compass or pair of pointed scissors (careful now!)

What you do:
1 Open the compass or scissors until
the points are about 2 mm apart.
2 Get your body to close its eyes
and gently touch a fingertip with
the points.
3 Order your body to open its eyes
and touch the skin of a calf (that's
the back of your body's lower leg
rather than a baby cow) with the
points.

You should find:
Your body senses two points touching
its finger, but only ONE POINT when
the points touch its calf! Fingers
are more sensitive than legs because
the touch sensors are closer
together. Yes, this experiment
really does make sense — I'm sure
you'll see the *point* of it.

SOUND, TASTE AND SCENT-DETECTOR SYSTEMS

Your body's audio-detector system registers sounds that are picked up by the external sound-detector dishes (or ears) mounted on each side of your head. The ear mechanism is engineered to turn sounds into nerve signals that go to your brain.

HOUSE WITH SATELLITE DISH

HEAD WITH SOUND DISH

But although your ears collect sound, you may be surprised to know that your body can detect sounds quite well *without them.* That's why bodies equipped with huge flapping ears aren't better at sound detection than those with smaller ears.

BODY DATA

1 In 1994 a Spanish body owner was having problems with his nagging mother-in-law. He sliced his own ears off in a bid to block the sound only to find out that it made little difference. So he had to listen to even more cutting remarks from his mother-in-law.

2 Your body's sound-detection system can't make out really high sounds such as bat squeaks. Mind you, some younger bodies have trouble detecting the words "go to bed now!"

FOOD AND AIRBORNE CHEMICAL SENSOR SYSTEMS

Your body's food chemical sensors are based on your tongue. That's the common name for the wobbly extensible probe located in your food-entry hatch and linked by nerves to your brain.

The smell/scent/whiff/pong detecting function is based in

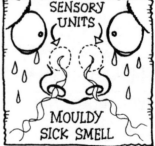

SENSORY UNITS

MOULDY SICK SMELL

the nose space. Here, two stamp-sized sensory units detect airborne chemicals and send nerve signals to your brain. You might be amazed to read that your brain's built-in memory files can store details of up to TEN THOUSAND smells – including revolting ones. Female bodies have more sensitive noses than male bodies. (This can cause problems if the male body gets sweaty and smelly.)

The sense of smell switches off if the nose sniffs one smell for hours and hours. I find it horribly hard to detect the odour of rotting flesh unless I take a horrible holiday from work, ha ha!

TEST YOUR BODY 3: THE STRANGE SECRET OF THE NOSTRILS

You will need:
- Your body
- A mirror

What you do:
1 Order your body to lift up its chin and use the mirror to take a good hard look up those nostrils — yes, I'm sorry folks, it's all in the name of science!
2 Make your body breathe sharply though the nostrils.

You should find:
The nostrils get bigger as your body takes in air, but one nostril is always slightly wider than the other. The smaller nostril often gets blocked when your body has been attacked by germs and has the disease known as a cold. (A disease is a minor body breakdown caused by germs. See page 139 for the drippy details.)

BODY SCENT DETECTION QUIZ

So how well do you know your own body? Are you a budding body expert or a baffled body beginner? Find out in the first of our series of exclusive body owner's quizzes...

1 Some body advice experts (known as doctors) detect diseases by sniffing the skin. What does gangrene (when the infected body bits rot) smell like?
a) School dinner.
b) Very old fish.
c) Mouldy apples.

2 In 2001, US military planners were working on extra-powerful stink bombs to control riots. In tests, what smell proved the most effective?
a) Poo (that's solid body waste, as if you didn't know!).
b) Sweaty feet smeared with rotting butter.
c) Vomit (ejected body food).

3 In the USA, fir trees are sprayed with a substance to put off thieves. What does this stinking substance smell like?
a) Skunk juice.
b) Fox wee.
c) Bad breath.

4 A sensory analyst is trained to spot dozens of different smells. In one US company women analysts were given a disgusting duty. Did they have to...?
a) Sniff the difference between old socks and maggoty cheese.
b) Sniff sweaty, dirty, smelly male armpits.
c) Sit by a smelly pond and sniff out foul-smelling frogs.

ANSWERS
1 c) Gangrene smells like mouldy apples. The disease typhoid smells like baking bread and yellow fever smells like fresh meat. Anyone fancy

a meaty sandwich with freshly baked bread? Er, thought not.

2 a) According to scientist Pam Dalton, who led the stink-bomb project, an ultra-powerful pooey pong made volunteers scream and curse, especially when mixed with rotting onions. Huh — what wimps! Have they never ventured into a school toilet?

3 b) The thieves were cutting down the trees and selling them as Christmas trees — it just wasn't "fir"! People didn't want trees that smelled of wee, so the tree thieves were foxed.

4 b) Sensory analysts train their noses to spot dozens of different smells. In one US company the women had to sniff the sweaty armpits of male bodies to test if a deodorant was working. I bet that job got up their noses!

And, speaking of sweating, the runny wet stuff that drips from your body when it's hot is yet another amazing automatic feature.

THE AMAZING AUTOMATIC BODY-COOLING SYSTEM

Your body is programmed to keep its inside temperature at about 37°C – that's the temperature at which it runs best. When your body heats up, three million micro-engineered units in the skin produce a watery fluid known to body owners as sweat. Sweat draws heat from the blood onto the skin and, as it dries, your body loses heat into the air.

WELL DONE, DAD. YOU MADE IT!

NO SWEAT!

SLICE THROUGH SKIN

HEAT   SWEAT

HAIR

SWEAT GLAND

Curious case study: A nose for danger

Your body sweats more when your brain senses danger. In the 1970s, British Intelligence body experts planned to use this fact to catch spies ... with the help of *gerbils*.

The plan involved setting up fans at airports. The fans wafted whiffs from passengers towards a gerbil's cage. The experts hoped the gerbil's sensitive snout would sniff the salty sweat of scared spies. And then someone spoilt the secret spy-spotters' secret scheme. They pointed out that every body sweats in airports – even if they've done nothing wrong! In other words, the plan really stinks!

If your body's skin-temperature sensors detect cold air, it switches on a completely different automatic programme. Your body is designed to automatically twitch its muscle power units – a movement known as shivering. The muscle motors give off heat as they work and this helps to keep your body warm.

A MESSAGE TO BODY OWNERS...

Now you've checked your body's automatic features, you might think that it does everything for itself. BIG MISTAKE! As I said in the Introduction, human bodies need lots of looking after, and that means YOU need a care routine. But don't panic, body owners! Your *Body Owner's Handbook* is bulging with brilliant body-care hints – starting in the next chapter!

BODY CARE FOR BODY OWNERS

WARNING!
Your body has NO guarantee...

Most things you buy have guarantees. Toasters and tea makers, electric nostril-hair pluckers and automatic bum-scratchers come with a piece of paper promising that if there's a fault, your machine will be repaired or you'll get a brand-new one. You may very well grumble — but this deal *isn't* on offer for your human body...

So you see, body owners, you've got to look after your body properly. I mean, if it breaks down, you'll find getting hold of a new body is harder than juggling custard. And that's why you really do need a body-care routine. But before we go into details, let's find out how NOT to do it…

In the bad old days before this handbook was written, some body owners dreamt up weird and wacky body-care routines. Our next curious case study is just one example amongst thousands…

Curious case study: Horrible health habits!

How mad is your mum? Well, compared to the Countess of Noailles I bet she's nearly normal. Back in Victorian times the crazy Countess inflicted her batty body-care beliefs on her adopted daughter, Maria. Poor Maria was sent to boarding school, and I bet she had to put up with letters like this one ...

To Maria Pasqua
The Convent School

My Dearest Darling Daughter
    I hope you're well and working hard at school. And I hope that Daisy the cow is well too! Now don't forget breathing cow farts is good for you. So tie Daisy up at night with her rear end sticking in through your bedroom window. Then you can breathe her lovely poopy bottom gas all night long! In the morning you should drink Daisy's

milk. Yes – drink it as it squirts from her udder straight into your mouth. As I always say, a healthy body is a happy body!

Now before I forget, dearest, I read your letter. I'm sorry the other girls make fun of you. Yes I did order you to go to school dressed as an Ancient Greek! But I'm sure they'll stop teasing you when they catch colds and you don't because of all that healthy freezing air wafting around your body! Not that there's much danger of colds since I made the school drain the pond. Ponds - Ugh! Nasty green

stinky things - just the sort of places germs breed! But, my dear, if you're still worried, the best way to keep germs at bay is to hang onions in your bedroom and wrap a dead cat around your neck. It worked for me!

Well, my dearest, that's all for now, but I'll write tomorrow with 164 more pages of health advice...

Your loving and health-conscious Mum,

 The Countess of Noailles

PS And don't forget to wear your healthy open-toed sandals!

Now you might think that the Countess had a few brain cells less than a headless chicken – and you'd be right! But, fortunately, this handbook has all the advice you need to take you through a whole day of sensible body-owning...

BODY CARE TIPS FOR BODY OWNERS
WAKING UP

Your body is programmed to wake up automatically at roughly the same time each day. Your brain automatically senses the light falling on your eyelids and switches to full-power mode as the light becomes brighter. You may like to try stretching your body to test its muscle motor power units and check they haven't become cramped during the night.

THE TOILET SHUFFLE

Once your body is woken up it has to be shuffled to the toilet in order to commence the liquid waste expulsion procedure known as peeing. At this point your body may not be alert enough to close to the door. Human bodies are designed to squirt out unwanted pee at regular intervals and your body will have a full bladder store of pee from the night.

Your bladder is fitted with sensors that send nerve signals to the brain as it stretches and fills up with pee. Actually, body owners should know that it's a good idea to let their body pee before the bladder gets too full. This saves the bladder from becoming too stretched and leaking at embarrassing moments.

BODY DATA

1 Pee is a deeper yellow in the morning because it contains several hours' worth of urea.

2 You may find it easier to order your body to stop breathing whilst peeing. This holds your diaphragm down and puts pressure on your bladder. Some bodies find it difficult to pee whilst taking deep breaths.

ALL-OVER BODY-CLEANING ROUTINE

Body owners don't agree on how often all-over body cleaning should take place. Some older body owners have a daily all-over body wash routine, but certain younger body owners think that NEVER is often enough!

I give the Monster *fourteen* baths a week — he gets horribly grubby grovelling in graveyards for body bits. After the bath, a quick squirt of Monster body scent gives him that horrible "just buried" aroma ...

Eau de Coffine

In fact, the number of times your body will need all-over cleaning depends on how dirty or sweaty it gets. You can wash off unwanted germs and sweat with soap and water. But soap stings your eyes and in the morning it's a good idea to wipe sleepy dust from these sensitive regions using a damp cloth.

After you've washed your body you should take extra care to dry the area between your toes so that the athlete's foot fungus won't grow and damage the skin.

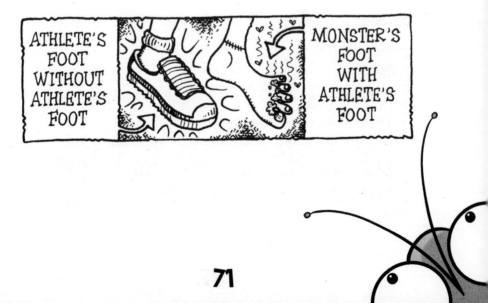

ATHLETE'S FOOT WITHOUT ATHLETE'S FOOT

MONSTER'S FOOT WITH ATHLETE'S FOOT

BODY DATA

Scientist Christina Agapakis and artist Sissel Tolaas invented new types of cheese using bacteria germs taken from their own bodies. They made creamy cheese with armpit and toe germs and a snot-yellow crumbly cheese with germs that lived in their noses. Fancy a nibble?!

HAIR-CLEANING ROUTINE

It's a smart idea for body owners to build a hair-washing session into their all-over body washing routine. Afterwards you can separate and smooth down the wet hair using a brush. Body owners shouldn't brush wet hair too hard – this splits the ends of the hairs and can turn a cool hairstyle into a frizzy fright wig…

BODY DATA

Before modern shampoos, body owners often used egg yolks to wash fair hair. The aim was shiny hair but sulphur chemicals in the egg triggered a chemical reaction that turned bleached blond hair green.

EAR-CLEANING ROUTINE

Ear-cleaning is a delicate part of your body cleaning routine. Your sensitive ear drums are located just a few centimetres into your ear holes. The ear drums pass on sounds to your hearing system but they're easily damaged. So if water gushes into an earhole, 'ears what to do.

1 Let it dry.

2 Gently wipe the *outside* of the ear with a clean cloth.

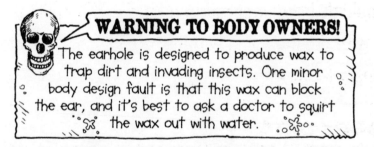

WARNING TO BODY OWNERS!

The earhole is designed to produce wax to trap dirt and invading insects. One minor body design fault is that this wax can block the ear, and it's best to ask a doctor to squirt the wax out with water.

NOSE-CLEANING PROCEDURE

Oh dear, the Monster's lost his handkerchief. "Monster, don't you DARE…!"

I apologize for the Monster's revolting behaviour just then! Here is the *correct* (and less disgusting) way to clean snot from your nose.

1 Blow one nostril at a time gently into a handkerchief whilst pinching the other shut.

2 Gently wipe the nostril.

NAIL CARE FOR BODIES

Body owners need to cut their finger and toe nails to stop them getting disgustingly long (younger body owners may need the help of an older body owner). The correct way to cut your nails is straight across so there's no danger of the nail cutting into your skin as it gets longer.

This is a vital but unpleasant job – and you really *wouldn't* want to know what the Monster gets under his fingernails. Watch out for low-flying nail-clippings!

REFUELLING YOUR BODY

Refuelling your body is another vital body-care procedure. You need to do it three times a day – in the morning, midday and evening. Without these vital pit stops your body suffers power loss and your brain begins to run data images of juicy hamburgers and succulent pizzas – and, oh dear, the monster's dribbled all over this page.

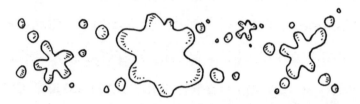

The most vital refuelling stop is the morning one: after your brain wakes up, it's groggy because it runs on a type of sugar called glucose. After a long night, your body's glucose levels are low. Why not treat your body to a glass of fruit juice? The juice contains glucose and a similar sugar to power up your brain.

The next step is the morning solid-food refuelling stop – the technical term for this is eating breakfast. You can tell when your body needs refuelling because your brain has a built-in fuel-level sensor for glucose levels in the blood. The sensor is known as appetite and when it registers when your body is low on glucose it's called hunger or feeling a bit peckish or even FEED ME NOW, I'M FLIPPING STARVING!

The Monster's signs of hunger are growling guts, plundering the pantry and chewing the cat

BREAKFAST MENU FOR MONSTER

TWO SOFT-BOILED EYEBALLS

TOAST FINGERS (USE BREAD FINGERS IF YOU CAN'T GET REAL ONES)

MUG OF HOT BLOOD

NICE KITTY!

Older body owners often fuel their bodies on tea or coffee in the morning. These drinks make certain body bits work faster because they contain a chemical called caffeine (caff-feen). Caffeine speeds up the heartbeat and the brain functions. But this uses up glucose and can leave the poor old bod trying to run on lower fuel levels later on.

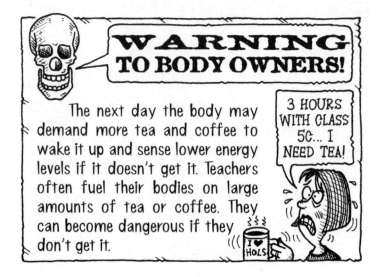

WARNING TO BODY OWNERS!

The next day the body may demand more tea and coffee to wake it up and sense lower energy levels if it doesn't get it. Teachers often fuel their bodies on large amounts of tea or coffee. They can become dangerous if they don't get it.

3 HOURS WITH CLASS 5C... I NEED TEA!

I ♥ HOLS

Curious case study: Death by coffee

Body experts once thought that coffee and tea contained poisons that built up in the body. One day, Swedish King Gustav III (1746–1792) decided to test this theory on two criminals.

It's a fact that a few cups of tea or coffee won't damage your body, although if they're taken at night they may keep your brain awake. And caffeine does widen your blood vessels. More blood goes to your kidneys and they make extra pee.

TOOTH-CLEANING TECHNIQUES

After refuelling your body it's time to clean your built-in food processors, known as teeth. Teeth are great for grinding and cutting your food but, unlike your eyeballs, they don't have a self-cleaning programme. This means that you, the body owner need to clean your teeth after body refuelling sessions.

This is a vital job because your mouth contains ONE HUNDRED MILLION MICROBES. Within minutes of refuelling, the microbes are gobbling food on your teeth. Worse still, they make acid that dissolves the super-tough enamel coating on your teeth and smelly gases that cause bad breath. The microbes are especially fond of sweet foods and they just love foods that glue themselves to your teeth to make a microbe holiday hideaway. And so, body owners, that's why you really do need to clean those teeth after fuelling your body on sweet foods.

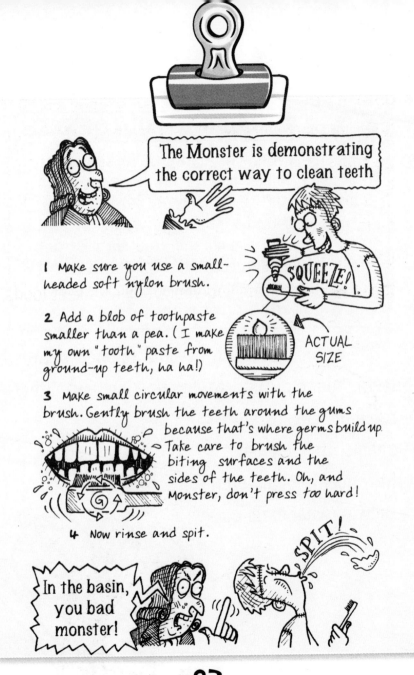

The Monster is demonstrating the correct way to clean teeth

1 Make sure you use a small-headed soft nylon brush.

SQUEEZE!

2 Add a blob of toothpaste smaller than a pea. (I make my own "tooth" paste from ground-up teeth, ha ha!)

ACTUAL SIZE

3 Make small circular movements with the brush. Gently brush the teeth around the gums because that's where germs build up. Take care to brush the biting surfaces and the sides of the teeth. Oh, and Monster, don't press too hard!

4 Now rinse and spit.

SPIT!

In the basin, you bad monster!

Bits of food can also become trapped *between* teeth. You may like to try flossing away these revolting remains. Once again, the Monster has been volunteered to show us what to do...

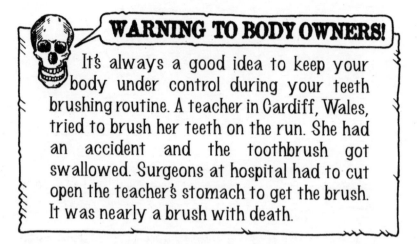

Now listen carefully, Monster

1 Take a 50 cm length of floss and wind the ends around your fingers.

2 Starting at one end, gently pass the floss between your teeth.

NEW STUFF!

3 When you've finished each tooth, wind the floss along.

WHAT A LIFE!

4 Afterwards you may throw the floss away, or use it to tie up the cat, ha ha!

I bet you never knew that some mouth microbes are killed by oxygen? They're descended from the earliest life-forms on Planet Earth over three billion years ago! When you floss, oxygen in the air reaches them and kills them. And no, just because they've been around for a long time it doesn't mean that they should be lovingly protected and preserved in a museum. So get brushing, body owners!

BODY DATA

A survey in 2000 showed that three-quarters of British body owners didn't know how to brush their teeth properly. And 13% of British bodies didn't have any teeth to brush, by gum!

OUT AND ABOUT WITH YOUR BODY

Older body owners are spot on – you really do need to wrap up well when it's a bit nippy. This is because your body can quickly lose heat in cold conditions. Despite your hair, your body loses up to 10% of its warmth through your head. This means that a hat is a useful item of body-warming equipment.

As your body gets colder it saves heat not by cutting down on the blood it sends to your brain but by reducing the supply to your fingers and toes. Without a fuel supply the cells break down. After a few days, the damaged body bits suffer gangrene – they turn black and drop off. Now can anyone remember what this *smells* like?

CLUES

IT ISN'T THIS...

AND IT ISN'T THIS!

Such a senseless waste of Monster spare parts! Wearing a hat stops heat loss from the head and keeps the blood warm. And it saves me having to sew the Monster's toes back on, ha ha!

HAT SEWN ON TO STOP IT BLOWING OFF

Obviously back strains are bad news for your body and sensible body owners train their body to walk and sit with a straight spine. This is the best position to protect the curve of your back and avoid back strains. If you train your body to hold its head up – the rest of your body should take up the correct position.

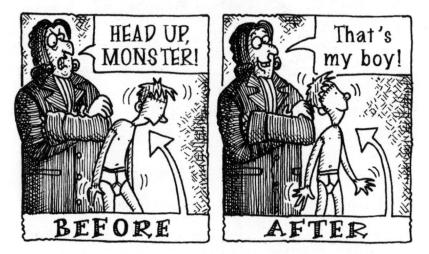

As a body owner you might be more than amazed to hear that walking bodies use only 40% of their energy in walking and waste 60% in lost heat from the muscles. (So *that's* why feet get so horribly hot and sweaty!) To use energy most effectively, your body needs to walk with its feet straight…

AVOIDING BACK DAMAGE

When your body is sitting for a long time, there's a risk of back strain. That's why you should take care to sit your body down on a chair that supports its lower back. Caring body owners could use a cushion to support this vital area…

Now the Monster will demonstrate the wrong and right way to lift a weight from the floor…

BENDING THE BACK CAN CAUSE MUSCLE STRAINS THAT TAKE THE BODY A LONG TIME TO REPAIR!	1 SQUAT YOUR BODY DOWN...	2 USE THE HANDS TO GRASP THE OBJECT LIKE SO	3 STRAIGHTEN YOUR BODY'S LEGS TO LIFT THE OBJECT

BODY DATA

If you happen to own a female body you need to know that high heels cause back problems if they're worn too often. The heels make your body walk off-balance and this results in back strain.

BODY SHUT-DOWN MODE

Your body needs time in shut-down mode in order to rest – body owners in the know call this "sleep", "forty winks" or "a nice snooze". Sleep normally takes place on a horizontal body recliner known as a bed. The bed should be firm enough to support your back, with a firm pillow for the head. (That way your head won't drop off before the rest of your body, ha ha!)

And now at last it's the Monster's bedtime...

Soaking your body in a nice hot bath is a great way to relax tired muscles. But eating a big meal three hours beforehand can delay the start of shutdown mode. Once your body is asleep, only basic activities such as digestion and breathing continue. Over the next few hours your body cools by 1°C and every two hours your brain automatically re-processes sensory information data (this is known as dreaming).

BODY DATA

Most dreams are in colour, but your brain often forgets the colours and retains only the boring black and white images in its memory systems. Mind you, if the dream was about a zebra that turned into a penguin I guess it wouldn't make much difference.

A fully-grown body needs seven or eight hours sleep to function properly. Smaller bodies need about nine to 12 hours. Your body is programmed to spend 22 years in shut-down mode. Fortunately, this doesn't happen all at once – well, not usually...

Curious case study: Sleeping Beauty

Sweden, 1876

Carolina Olsson lay on her narrow bunk and wished that her head would stop hurting. She had bashed her head a few days earlier, and it was still sore.

It was all she could do to stay awake.

Why did she feel so tired?

Carolina thought about her family and their little cottage and how she used to love to tell her brothers about her dreams. But her thoughts were in a whirl. She closed her eyes ... and slept. She slept all day and all night. When Carolina didn't wake up her family called the doctor.

The old doctor scratched his head and yelled "WAKE UP!" But Carolina didn't stir. The doctor looked grim. He produced a pin and jabbed it into the girl's hand. No reaction. The doctor shook his head and mumbled that he didn't know what was wrong. Doctors at the hospital gave Carolina electric shocks – they didn't work either. And more time passed.

Then, one fine spring day, Carolina opened her eyes. Feeling weak and dizzy, she stood up and called for her mum. But her mum didn't come. Instead a stranger – an old woman shuffled into the room. The old woman's mouth fell open and her little blue eyes nearly popped from their sockets.

"Bless you, dear, you're awake at last!" she declared.

"Where's Mum?" asked Carolina in alarm.

The old woman shook her head. She gripped Carolina's wrist in her bony hand.

"You'd better sit down, dear," she said. "You've been asleep for a very long time."

"What do you mean?" asked Carolina, sitting down.

"Your poor mother passed away four years ago. Two of your bothers drowned in an accident."

Carolina felt cross and confused. Who was this old witch? Why was she telling such terrible lies? The old woman tottered to the door and called Carolina's father and two surviving brothers.

"Come quick!" she screeched. "She's awake!"

Three strangers appeared and they stared at Carolina in amazement. Carolina stared back. Her brothers were grown up and her father was old and grizzled with a grey beard. Carolina began to cry – why was everyone so old? What was this cruel trick they were playing? Were they all under the witch's spell?

Gently, the old woman explained the terrible truth. Carolina had slept for 32 years. She wasn't fourteen any more – she was 46 years old. Carolina's mum had fed her daughter on milk and sugar to keep her alive. When Carolina's mum died the old woman took over the job.

Carolina was thin but healthy and the newspapers called her "Sleeping Beauty" because she looked so young for her age. She lived a long and happy life but there was one thing she never talked about – one secret she would never share. She never told anyone the dreams that filled her strange and enchanted sleep.

BODY DATA

Modern body experts can't explain Carolina's long sleep. After certain types of head injury the brain can shut down for years. This is called a coma – but it's very unusual for a lengthy coma to end in a full recovery.

And now it's time to pull all the bits of this chapter together. The Baron has kindly supplied a checklist for all the body-care hints in these pages…

THE BARON'S DAILY BODY-CARE CHECKLIST

▶Morning: Wake up and stretch body.

▶Visit toilet. ▶Wash, bath or shower: don't forget ear care, nail care, hair care. ▶Drink to wake up brain (but not too much coffee or tea).

▶Get dressed. ▶Refuel body (breakfast). ▶Wrap up warm if going out in cold weather. ▶Out and about (don't forget how to walk and sit and lift properly). ▶Refuel body (lunch). ▶Out and about again. ▶Refuel body (supper). ▶Wash, bath or shower. ▶Go to bed. ▶Sleep.

And now it's time for your body to tiptoe into the next chapter. But, before we move on, I ought to point out that we've missed one of the most vital body-care questions. Choosing the right fuel for your body. Oh well, I'm sure you'll devour the next few pages…

BOOSTING YOUR BODY

There's one thing your human body machine does that's truly amazing: it builds itself. Unlike every other machine on Earth, it actually gets bigger and stronger in its first 20 years! This means that clued-up body owners can create their own high-performance bodies! But first you'll need to know about the two F's, FUEL and FITNESS. Yes, read on for the full fuel and fitness facts...

FUELLING YOUR BODY

As you know, food is your body's fuel. Food energy helps your body function and grow and repair damage and move around. But what's the best type of fuel to use? There's a confusing choice of body fuels on offer…

No wonder body owners can get really worried about refuelling! They really do get their knickers in a twist…

AM I PUTTING IN TOO MUCH FUEL?

OR TOO LITTLE?

IS IT THE RIGHT KIND OF FUEL?

OR THE WRONG KIND?

TWIST!

KNICKERS

Hey, r-e-l-a-x! As I said, your brain's fuel-sensor detects hunger, and sensors in the stomach tell the brain when it's full. Your body consumes about 50 tonnes of food in its lifetime, but not all at once!

All you do is fuel up your body when it's hungry and stop fuelling when the stomach signals that it's full. In fact, your body will feel more hungry in cold weather or when it's active because it needs extra energy to keep warm and keep moving. It's also a good idea to top up your body with water or liquid fuel. This means drinking to replace water lost as sweat from the automatic cooling system. You will probably find that your body needs more drinks in hot weather when it's soaking with sweat.

> ## WARNING TO BODY OWNERS!
> Too much water can damage your body. If a body is given more than a hundred litres in two hours, it pees non-stop and loses the vital salts it needs to send nerve signals. This can actually cause total body breakdowns, but it's very unusual.

TYPES OF BODY FUEL

You can group body fuels in the following way…

• Carbohydrate foods – your body can break down these foods into sugars such as glucose. They can be used to power your muscles.

• Sugar-rich foods – provide an instant glucose energy fuel-boost for your body.

- Protein-rich foods – useful for building new cells as part of your body's unique self-repair and growing program.

- Fatty foods – useful for topping up your body's long-term portable reserve fuel tanks, otherwise known as fat.

- Roughage – that's fruit and vegetable skins, leaves, seeds, bran from wholemeal bread, etc. Roughage isn't a fuel but it's useful for digestion. (See page 125 to find out why, but be warned – it's a bit rude!)

Still not sure what the best body fuel is? Well, you'll need to give your body all those listed to maintain high performance. You can combine them in lots of ways – why not try making this high-quality fuel booster (also known as a snack)?

TEST YOUR BODY 4: GETTING A-HEAD

You will need:
- A slice of wholemeal bread
- A sliced hard-boiled egg
- Some cress
- A sliced tomato
- Butter or margarine

IMPORTANT NOTE: Younger body owners should ask an older body owner to do the chopping and boiling and slicing. After all, the recipe doesn't need chopped, boiled, or sliced *fingers*.

What you do:
1 Lay the bread on a plate and spread a little butter or margarine on it. I say "a little" because your body doesn't need too much fat.
2 Arrange the cress as "hair" at the top of the slice.
3 Use two slices of egg as "eyes".
4 Cut a slice of tomato in half to make a sad or happy mouth.
5 Scoff the lot!

You should find:
The head contains all the food fuels your body needs. The bread contains carbohydrates, the egg has protein, the butter has fat and the bread, tomato and cress contain roughage.

BODY DATA

In the 1980s, US scientist Bernd Heinrich was keen to boost his body's running performance. So he fuelled his body on 600 ml of honey. Bees can fly miles on a drop of honey so it made sense for Bernd's body – right? Wrong! The honey caused dreadful diarrhoea. And the only running record Bernd broke was DASHING TO THE LOO!

There! Everything a body owner needs to know about food without wasting vast amounts of money on the sort of useless reduced body refuelling schedule (known as a diet) that you find in glossy body owner's magazines…

To sum up: all you need to remember is to refuel your body three times a day on a range of body fuels. And your brilliant body does the rest! Well, that wasn't too hard too swallow, was it? And now it's time to... Oh, hold on! I'm getting loads of emails from body owners. It seems I've left out one terribly important fact...

Dear Body Owner's Handbook Author

Is chocolate good for my body? PLEASE TELL ME IT IS, PLEASE, PLEASE – p-leeeeeeeze!

Irma Despereet

Well, Irma, the average body guzzles 3,200 chocolate bars in its life, so this is an important question. Yes, OK, hold on, I'm giving you the answer. Please *listen*!

1 Fuelling your body on chocolate makes your brain churn out powerful chemicals called endorphins (en-dorf-fins). Endorphins are usually made to block the "pain" nerve signals that your body sends to your brain when it's damaged. The chemicals trigger the brain data programme known as happiness. So choccie cheers up your brain. Happy so far?

2 Choccie also contains caffeine, which makes your brain feel more awake, and other substances that lower blood pressure by widening the blood vessels and thinning the blood. This helps the blood flow more quickly through the blood vessels. Sounds really good, doesn't it?

3 So feeding your body PLAIN chocolate (without the fat-containing milk) about *once a week* is good for it… Oh dear!

Well, I'm sorry if you want to feed your body milk chocolate 25 times a day! Hey, don't blame me, I'm only the author! Hmm, methinks I'd better change the subject…

HOW TO REFUEL YOUR BODY

Oddly enough, after all the fuss about what kind of fuel to put in their bodies, most body owners aren't too bothered about how it actually gets *inside* their body. But body owners need to know what happens – for one thing, it can all go *horribly* wrong!

Most of the time the job is done automatically, as the Monster will demonstrate using a bowl of foul-smelling dog food that the dog didn't want…

X-RAY VIEW OF MONSTER EATING DOG FOOD

1 The Monster's teeth mash the food as spit squirts into his mouth. They work at a speed of 129 metres an hour.

2 The Monster's tongue shoves the food to the back of his mouth.

3 The epiglottis (the lid of the windpipe) snaps into place to stop the food slithering the wrong way to his lungs.

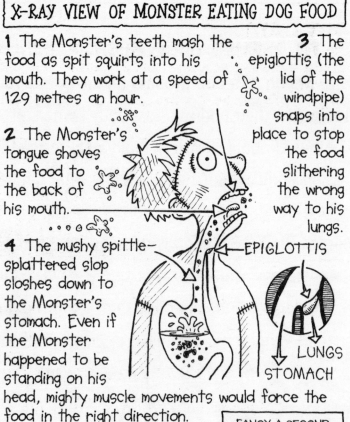

EPIGLOTTIS

4 The mushy spittle-splattered slop sloshes down to the Monster's stomach. Even if the Monster happened to be standing on his head, mighty muscle movements would force the food in the right direction.

LUNGS

STOMACH

5 The one-way trip takes nine to thirteen seconds at a speed of 61 metres an hour. In fact, the Monster could polish off another bowl of food before the first one splashes into his squelching stomach juices.

FANCY A SECOND HELPING, MONSTER?

NO THANKS!

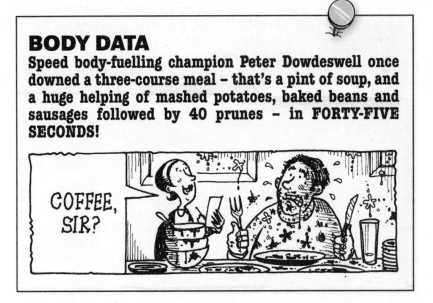

COFFEE, SIR?

Fast-fuelling sounds fun doesn't it? Unfortunately it can lead to noisy gas escapes from the mouth and the rear gas vent/solid waste ejection pipe. These embarrassing incidents are known as "burping" and "farting". The gas consists of air swallowed with food and gas made by gut microbes that feed on the food. If the food hasn't been properly chewed, it won't be well-digested and the microbes will make more gas. Some of these gases are very smelly and body owners should avoid releasing them in lifts, public transport or posh restaurants – and especially not with sound effects.

Another fast-fuelling problem is that acid can gush up from your stomach – this is known as indigestion or heart burn. Whatever you call it – it's a pain in the guts for your body!

SPEEDY HICCUPS

Fast-fuelling bodies can also suffer from a condition in which the diaphragm twitches uncontrollably – the technical term for this is hiccups. (The diaphragm pulls down to help your body breathe, remember?) Hiccups are said to happen because nerve signals are confused by fast eating. To prove this, the Baron has given the Monster a live frog to eat.

If your body goes into hiccup mode you could try stopping the automatic breathing mechanism – this is called "holding your breath". Carbon dioxide builds up in your blood, slowing the twitching nerves and halting the hiccups. A drink has a similar effect because your body has to hold its breath in order to swallow.

111

OK, so maybe fast-fuelling is a bad idea, but there's no need for slow-fuelling either. In 1903 body expert Horace Fletcher claimed that food should be chewed hundreds of times. To prove his point Fletcher sent poo samples to body experts. The experts weren't impressed. I guess they poo-poohed the whole idea.

BODY DATA

1 It's a good idea to keep your body under control whilst swallowing. Singing, talking, giggling or farmyard impressions can result in food going down the wrong way. And this activates your body's air tube clearing procedure, known as "coughing and spluttering".

2 A blocked air tube can result in a body emergency known as "choking". In 1994 Mexican entertainer Ramón Barrero suffered total body breakdown after choking on the world's smallest mouth organ. It must have been no choke, I mean no joke for the musical Mexican.

Now at this point you might well be wondering what happens to the food that your body has been so busily refuelling itself on. Well, if you've read this far you'll know that your guts break up chemicals in your food so they can pass into your blood. (Check back to page 26 if you've just joined us.)

And from now on it all gets rather scientific. Er, so what happens next, Baron?

BODY LANGUAGE

It's about ATP!

The Baron's talking about a teepee tent? That must be a creepy teepee, tee hee!

ANSWER

The Baron says… No, you foolish reader! ATP[1] is your body's energy store. The body's cells use breathed-in oxygen to turn chemicals in glucose or other foods into ATP. The body uses ATP to power its muscles and the vital chemical reactions that make the body function and grow. The process of turning food into energy is called respiration. The waste carbon-dioxide gas wheezes from the lungs, ha ha!

---

1 That's adenosine triphosphate (a-deen-o-sin try-fos-fate) if you really want to impress the Baron.

Thank you, Baron Frankenstein, and whilst we're talking about energy, this is a good time to introduce the topic we mentioned right at the start of this chapter. Anyone remember it? Hey, wake up, body owners – boosting your body needs more than just fuel, it needs FITNESS, and you know what that means?

IT'S WAKEY-WAKEY, WORK THAT BODY TIME!

All bodies need exercise and as a responsible body owner it's your job to make sure your body gets its fair share. Sadly not all body owners take their responsibilities seriously and some of them seem to be training for Couch Potato Olympics.

So why is this handbook keen on exercise? Why don't we say chill-out and choccie is better than getting in a sweat? Well, because it's not – and it's all to do with the way your body works. To explain why, let's compare your body to an automatic bum-scratching machine.

If you use your automatic bum-scratching machine ten times a day it's going to wear out sooner or later (especially if it's not up to scratch). But your body is different. Unlike the machine, you can't wear out your muscles by giving them lots of exercise – instead you actually make them BIGGER and STRONGER. And that of course makes your body stronger. That's the good news – the not-so-good news is your muscles get smaller and weaker if you don't exercise them.

Now this handbook is NOT about how to turn your body into a super-fit athlete/footballer or whatever-you'd-like-it-to-be. As far as looking after your body is concerned, the only rule is to get as much exercise as you can and eat healthily. I'll be back in a few seconds, but first the Baron wants to say something...

I am grimly determined that the Monster wins the Annual Monster's Cross-country Race. Yes, long nights have I brooded and plotted and yet I fear the opposition! Wolfman has four legs, Big Foot's long legs match his big feet, and the Mummy is wrapped up in his training. There is nothing for it — the Monster must take more exercise to become a stronger runner. MONSTER, FETCH MY WHIP!

WOLFMAN

BIGFOOT THE MUMMY

Hold it right there, Baron!

Exercise isn't about forcing your body to do anything. It's about fun! So why not treat your body to a new sport? How about cycling? Swimming is great since your body uses a wide range of muscles. Yes, as I said, have FUN with exercise. Unless you own a seriously sporty body, exercise is about grinning, not winning!

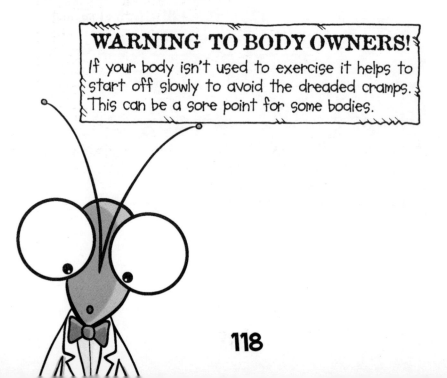

WARNING TO BODY OWNERS!

If your body isn't used to exercise it helps to start off slowly to avoid the dreaded cramps. This can be a sore point for some bodies.

BODY DATA

1 When your muscle cells try to make energy without enough oxygen, they make lactic acid instead. A rapid build-up of lactic acid can trigger cramp. This is more likely to happen in tired muscles that aren't used to exercise. Sounds like another reason to exercise doesn't it?

2 An American scientist decided to find out how much lactic acid lizards make when they run. He let a lizard have a run and plonked it in a food blender and ... yes, you've guessed the rest. He measured the acid in the souped-up lizard. Anyone for lizard soup?

WHAT A "SOUPER" EXPERIMENT!

SPLAT!

POOR FRED!

WARNING TO BODY OWNERS!

Body owners SHOULD NOT try this experiment on hamsters, stick insects, little brothers or any other small helpless creatures.

A sensible way to avoid cramps is to give your body a warm-up routine like the one the Monster is attempting...

TEST YOUR BODY 5: EXERCISE YOUR BODY
... WITHOUT LEAVING YOUR ARMCHAIR
You will need:
• Your body plus a friend's body.

What you do:
1 Ask your friend to read the
following instructions in any order
whilst your body tries to carry them
out. How fast can your friend read
and how fast can your body move?
2 Here are the instructions:

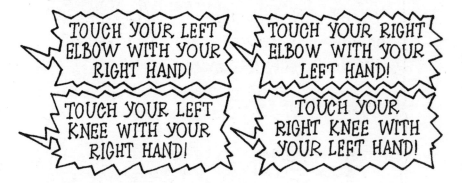

TOUCH YOUR LEFT ELBOW WITH YOUR RIGHT HAND!

TOUCH YOUR RIGHT ELBOW WITH YOUR LEFT HAND!

TOUCH YOUR LEFT KNEE WITH YOUR RIGHT HAND!

TOUCH YOUR RIGHT KNEE WITH YOUR LEFT HAND!

3 When you've had enough, swap over.
You read the instructions and see
how fast your friend's body manages
to carry them out.

You should find:
Your body can move at quite a speed, but
it's quite easy for the poor old brain
to get confused by the instructions.

So how did you get on? I hope your body's not too hot and sweaty and wrung out like an old dishcloth so that the stairs feel like Mount Everest. But if so, flop your body back into that cosy armchair and consider the really rich rewards of exercise...

THE REALLY RICH REWARDS OF EXERCISE
Regular exercise results in...

• More energy. OK, I know your body feels tired after exercise. But as your muscles grow bigger and stronger they'll have more energy. And that gives your body more get-up-and-go power.
• A stronger heart – like any muscle, your heart gets stronger as it beats faster with exercise. A strong heart means less risk of future problems – so body owners really need to take this advice to heart.
• A brainier brain. Body experts reckon that exercise makes your brain smarter. In some schools, children take exercise between

lessons and these children score more highly in tests. Just think — having a strong heart sends a stronger bloodflow to your brain. And this gets your brain working harder and faster.

• A good night's sleep. Exercising in the evening or late afternoon relaxes your body and helps it rest during sleep mode.

• Happiness — yes, exercise actually makes your brain feel happy! It releases those wonderful feel-good factor endorphins. So you see, exercise really is better than chocolate.

What d'ya mean you'll settle for chocolate?

Rejoice, dear readers! Thanks to exercise, the Monster is fit for the race. But is he fit to win? Time alone will tell...

A FEW NIGHTS LATER...

The bell tolled midnight. My heart beat wildly, so I put it back in its box, ha ha! The monsters took their places on the starting line...

BIG FOOT | MONSTER | MUMMY | WOLFMAN | ZOMBIES

The stupid zombies ran off in the wrong direction. Wolfman took the lead followed by Big Foot — Monster was last. Then Wolfman stopped to sniff a dead sheep and Big Foot stepped on a tin-tack. This left only the Mummy and sadly he began to unwind when someone trod on his bandages...

Of course, I had *nothing* to do with these accidents but I did help the Monster over the

I WANT MY MUMMY!

finishing line! Anyway ... we WON! And winning means everything to a mad scientist like me, whatever the author says!

Yeah, OK, Baron. And on that triumphant note we end this chapter ... but wait! I forgot to mention how the body gets rid of solid waste. Well, I suppose this body owner's handbook has to cover this vital job even though it's unpleasant and smelly. Maybe you should order your body to hold its nose...

SOLID-WASTE EJECTION PROCEDURE

All human bodies produce solid waste. This has many names, most of which are too rude for a respectable handbook like this one.

YOU MEAN LIKE, PLOP, POOP, BIG JOBS, NUMBER TWO'S...

YES, OK, OK. THAT'S QUITE ENOUGH!

The smelly waste is squeezed out of the rear-end gas vent/solid-waste ejection pipe about once a day. Roughage helps the guts grip the waste and move it on faster. Bodies fuelled on foods full of roughage can produce waste up to *seven times* a day.

Three facts about solid waste that body owners may prefer not to read before meals...

1 All those sit-down sessions on the toilet really do add up. Did you know that your body spends about six months of its life on the toilet? Mind you, that's a TOTAL of six months not six months non-stop on the toilet otherwise people will be banging on the door and asking what's going on in there.

2 Most body owners learn that poo smells disgusting when they're about two. But that didn't stop one woman from EATING poo! In 1731 she *ate* a plate of poo in Paris. She washed down the disgusting dish with a yellowish liquid that looked suspiciously like …. yes, you guessed it. She scoffed this sickening supper for religious reasons and let's *pray* that no one else does. And your family won't thank you for reading this bit aloud when the posh relations come for dinner.

3 Although poo was a subject that was left in the closet (literally), in 1994, Leeuwarden Museum in the Netherlands broke all the rules. The adverts might have looked like this…

Er, this might be a good moment for us to make our excuses and leave this chapter.

AUTOMATIC BODY-REPAIR SYSTEMS

Your body can get damaged by being knocked in some way or it can be attacked by germs. As you know, your body is designed to self-repair damage and destroy germs – but as a responsible body owner, you ought to know what's going on.

So now's the moment to introduce this handbook's very own body-advice expert: in the village of Much Moaning, Dr Grimgrave is a much-loved local physician who can't do enough for his patients.

I NEVER VISIT AT WEEKENDS. BY MONDAY THE PATIENT IS USUALLY BETTER ... OR DEAD!

MOTHER

OK, so I got that last bit wrong! The truth is that if Dr Grimgrave was your body-advice expert you'd get the MOT – that's "Miserable Offensive Treatment"! Anyway, before we hear more from Dr G, let's take a look at a bashed-up body and find out how it repairs itself.

BODY SELF-REPAIR SYSTEMS

The Baron has kindly agreed to show us his grisly old photo album of bodywork damage suffered by the Monster. (Sensitive readers may like to read this next bit with their eyes closed!)

Ah, the sweet innocence of youth! The Monster was always getting into fights with the zombies. I've got some lovely pictures in my foul photographic albums of the injuries he suffered, ha ha!

Bruises

When your body gets knocked, blood vessels under your skin can leak blood. The chemicals in the blood break apart, first appearing dark blue before turning to lovely shades of red, purple and yellow like a glorious sunset. White blood cells gobble up the leftovers and the bruise fades.

A black eye is a bruised eyelid...

A cauliflower ear is a swelling caused by a blood clot under the skin, not a large vegetable stuck to the side of the Monster's head.

What a clot!

Your body's automatic self-repair system switches on as soon as your skin gets cut or scratched. Thirteen blood chemicals form stringy fibres. These trap red blood cells and microscopic objects in the blood called platelets and create a clot.

You'll be pleased to read that the clot dries to form a fresh crusty scab. It's meant to keep germs out whilst your skin re-forms underneath from the edges of the wound. Well, that's the plan — but some young body owners pick their dead crunchy scabs and chew them!

But Dr Grimgrave isn't too pleased...

Bah! The little clots should be served scab sandwiches for their supper!
This revolting habit slows the body's healing.

The broken ends of bones also form clots before beginning to join together. That's why it's vital to keep broken bones straight. Once the bone has healed, special cells shape the healed area and make it as much like the old bone as possible.

BODY DATA
In the 1990s British surgeons tested a new glue to help fix broken bones. The strange substance contained blood mixed with crab poo. Claw-blimey!

SCARY SCARS

If the wound is big, your body plugs the gap with collagen. Collagen isn't skin, but as an emergency body covering it's up to the job. Mind you, it looks different and areas of collagen healing are known as scars. By the way, body owners shouldn't worry too much if their body picks up a few scars over the years. It's nice to keep your body in mint condition but a few scars are to be expected as it's hard for a body to avoid bumps and scrapes. Some body owners even think they give their bodies an interesting, rugged look.

BODY DATA

If you're worried about scars spoiling the look of your body you'll be glad to know that scientists tested spray-on skin in 2001. The spray contained the patient's own skin cells and was designed to cover wounds and speed up healing. Hmm – it sounds better than spray-on furniture polish. Spray that on and you'll end up with a long-lasting finish.

Curious case study: Bashed-up bodies

Your body is tougher than you think. Like all bodies, it's built to last. And some bodies have survived the most horrendous damage...

1 In 1984 an American boy had nearly all his skin burned off in a fire. Luckily, scientists were able to re-grow his skin from a few remaining scraps. Meanwhile the boy's body was wrapped in skin taken from dead bodies. He lived.

2 A Canadian lumberjack was chopping down a tree when his chainsaw slipped. He cut his WHOLE BODY IN HALF – except for nerves in his spine that took messages from his brain to his body. He made it home in one piece (not two pieces).

One problem with serious body damage or major bodywork repair jobs like those we've been talking about is that germs can creep into the body through the wounds. This is called an infection and the body owner may notice a watery substance oozing from the area. Body experts call this pus. Pus is the result of the body's germ defence system – er, hold on, the Baron is itching to tell you the disgusting details...

Ah, the sweet smell of fresh pus! Pus is an interesting mixture of liquid from blood, dead white blood cells and dead germs. Smelly brown pus means a serious infection, when limbs may need to be chopped off, ha ha! But a little pus seems to get the body's defences to work harder and the wound heals faster.

PUS ON PUSS

A NOTE FROM THE AUTHOR

The Baron has just offered to show us his book of home remedies. He says that he's tried most of them on the Monster, but I'm not sure if Dr Grimgrave approves of this sort of thing...

GRRR! THIS BOOK IS UTTER HOGWASH!

FATHER

BARON FRANKENSTEIN'S SECRET BOOK OF CURES

LICKING WOUNDS

When bloodied in a fight, all animals lick their wounds. The water helps to wash out dirt and the spit contains germ-killing substances. Sadly these do not kill all germs which is why the mouth oozes with microbes and I am told that doctors don't advise spitting on wounds.

LICK!

HARMFUL MICROBES

TO CLEAR UP AN INFECTED WOUND.
Pour a small bucket of squirming
maggots over the wound. Ah, my little
wriggling friends! Maggots devour rotten
flesh and help with the healing.
Modern doctors use maggots and the
Australian Ngemba tribe traditionally
used bandages
dripping with blood
and maggots for
the same reason.
How intriguing!

WRIGGLE!
MUNCH!
SQUIRM!
DON'T LEAVE THEM ON TOO LONG!

Note to myself: I must remember to
use blowfly maggots on the Monster.
African tumbu maggots burrow into
flesh. They may be removed by leaving
bacon on the skin and
yanking the maggots out
when they come out to feed.
Oh well, it might save the
Monster's bacon, ha ha!

TIME TO COME OUT!

Fortunately, if your body is unlucky enough to be attacked by germs you don't need to rely on the Baron's rotten remedies. Your automatic germ-destroying system is ready and waiting…

THE AUTOMATIC GERM-DESTROYING SYSTEM

Wide-awake readers of this handbook will know that skin and snot and tears form part of the body's defence systems. But if germs get inside your body they're zapped by your body's super-complex white blood cell defence system. Here's how it works…

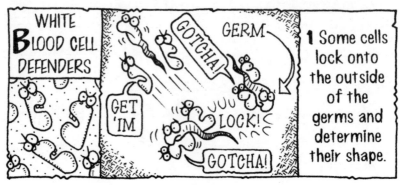

WHITE **B**LOOD CELL DEFENDERS

GOTCHA! GERM

GET 'IM

LOCK!

GOTCHA!

1 Some cells lock onto the outside of the germs and determine their shape.

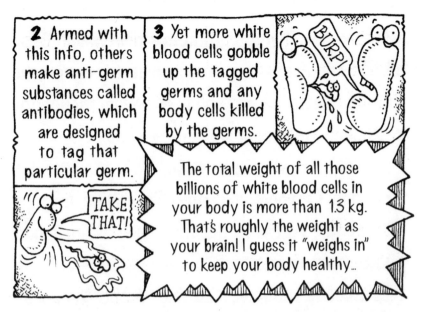

2 Armed with this info, others make anti-germ substances called antibodies, which are designed to tag that particular germ.

3 Yet more white blood cells gobble up the tagged germs and any body cells killed by the germs.

TAKE THAT!

BURP!

The total weight of all those billions of white blood cells in your body is more than 1.3 kg. That's roughly the weight as your brain! I guess it "weighs in" to keep your body healthy...

DISEASE ATTACKS ON SMALLER BODIES

Some smaller bodies get clobbered by any disease that's around. This is because their body defences aren't too good at fighting off germs. In fact, small bodies often pick up diseases from their local germ factory (sorry, I mean *school*).

Fortunately, small bodies are tough enough to recover quickly. In fact their anti-germ defences grow stronger because some of their white blood cells "remember" the germs and attack them next time. As a result younger body owners get sent back to school all too soon…

In 2000, Italian scientists claimed that a little dirt was good for younger bodies. By getting to grips with germs, body owners train their white blood cells to fight disease.

So making mud pies, getting slobber-kissed by the dog, licking fluffy lollies and other revolting activities may not be so bad. If you're a young body owner you might like to share this scientific info with the next grumpy adult who tells you off for getting mucky. Who says "grime doesn't pay"?

BODY DATA

1 Germs float through the air and land on your hands. And from your hands they get breathed in through your nose. That's why nose picking is a sure-fire way to get cold germs into your body. Your body feels sick and, of course, anyone who is watching feels even sicker.

2 Once a cold or flu (a more violent version of a cold) starts to develop, you need to drag your poorly body to bed. Sensible body owners fuel-up with plenty of liquids but you shouldn't try rubbing your chest with animal fat (this traditional Russian remedy does a fat lot of good). And wrapping a dead cat around your neck like the crazy Countless of Noailles won't have you "feline" better either.

3 One body fuel that might help is chicken soup. So said scientists at the University of Nebraska, USA in 2000. They reckoned the soup helps your body make extra snot. Since snot is part of your body's automatic anti-germ defences, the soup is good for colds. Mind you, I think it tastes *fowl*.

OK, so the message is crystal clear: your body is designed to heal itself. Most of the time it doesn't need help. But that hasn't stopped brainless body owners trying all sorts of daft DIY healing methods.

Of course they're as sensible as putting your pet poodle in a python's cage and saying "hope you guys don't mind sharing". But the Baron's an old-fashioned kind of mad scientist and he believes in this rubbish. And what's more, if I don't show you that dreadful old cure book he's going to chase me with his bone saw ...

BARON FRANKENSTEIN'S SECRET BOOK OF CURES

HOW TO TREAT A SORE THROAT USING PEE

There are two schools of thought about this. I think it works, and everyone else thinks it doesn't. Gargling with hot fresh pee is an ancient Chinese remedy. I tried it on the Monster once and he's never complained of a sore throat since!

NOT AS POTTY AS YOU MIGHT THINK

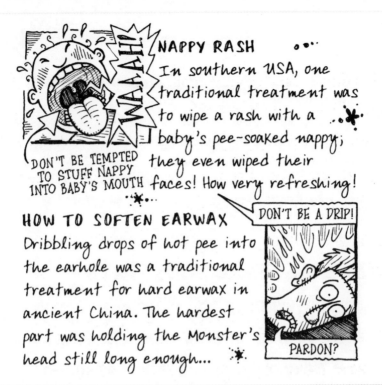

NAPPY RASH

In southern USA, one traditional treatment was to wipe a rash with a baby's pee-soaked nappy; they even wiped their faces! How very refreshing!

DON'T BE TEMPTED TO STUFF NAPPY INTO BABY'S MOUTH

HOW TO SOFTEN EARWAX

Dribbling drops of hot pee into the earhole was a traditional treatment for hard earwax in ancient China. The hardest part was holding the Monster's head still long enough...

DON'T BE A DRIP!

PARDON?

I am afraid Dr Grimgrave isn't too impressed by these treatments:

GRR! THESE SO-CALLED CURES ARE UTTER PIFFLE!

GRANDMA

BF'S

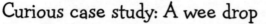

Curious case study: A wee drop

The urea in urine tastes terrible and it's poisonous in large doses but that hasn't put some barmy body owners off drinking pee. In the 1970s Indian Prime Minister Morarji Desai drank his own pee every day. So was he a potty PM? Some body owners think not! In 2013 ninety-one-year-old Mark Ambrose said that drinking the stuff kept his body youthful. What's more he dabbed his face with pee to speed up healing.

ORDERING SPARE BODY PARTS

If some of your body bits get worn out or damaged beyond repair, it's great to know that surgeons can remove many body bits and stick in spare parts from broken-down bodies. In fact, hospitals can get hold of replacement hearts, livers, kidneys, and even hands. I expect they come from a "second-hand" shop.

No, seriously, these spare parts are often given away freely once a body is beyond repair. But in the USA in 2001 people were selling body bits for money. Here are some actual body bit prices from that year. You may be amazed at how much a broken-down body is worth!

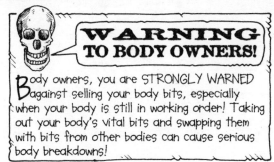

HONEST JOE'S USED BODS	YOU NEVER KNOW WHEN YOU MIGHT NEED THEM!
One cornea (the see-through bit of the eyeball)	£2,500
One set of bones	£19,500
0.37 square metres of skin	£26,000
Pick 'n' mix box of leftover body bits	£98,500
TOTAL COST OF BITS	£146,500

(Genuine body bits — one careful owner!)

WARNING TO BODY OWNERS!

Body owners, you are STRONGLY WARNED against selling your body bits, especially when your body is still in working order! Taking out your body's vital bits and swapping them with bits from other bodies can cause serious body breakdowns!

145

If you don't like the idea of bits from another body being put into your body, there is an alternative – use a machine designed for the job. Body experts are also developing ever-improved mechanical replacement body parts including joints, voice boxes and hearts.

BODY OWNER'S REPAIR QUIZ

So you've read this chapter and reckon you're a body repair expert? Well, if so you'll breeze through this queasy quiz. Which of these so-called body repair facts are just too stupid to be true?
Say TRUE or FALSE?
1 It's possible to have blue snot up your nose.
2 Hitting your head makes your brain see stars.
3 Reading wears out your eyeballs.
4 Injecting your body with pee helps it to fight germs.

ANSWERS

1 TRUE (in theory). Some bacteria are blue and snot oozing with the bacteria would be blue too. But you might see it once in a blue moon (or do I mean once in a blue hankie?). By the way, green snot gets its lovely colour from a germ-killing substance containing iron made by white blood cells. **2** TRUE. The blow switches on your body's retina light-detectors. They fire nerve signals and your brain thinks they're light flashes. **3** FALSE. Reading non-stop for hours can strain the muscles that hold your pupils open. (Pupils are the holes that allow light into your eyeballs.) But no amount of reading will "wear out" your eyeballs. Yes – you can eyeball this handbook in total safety! **4** FALSE. But in 1990, a doctor in California, USA got into trouble for injecting his patients with pee and making this claim.

So how did you do? Are you fit to be a body expert or is your state of knowledge rather sickly? Either way, you'll find plenty of riveting reading in the next chapter. It's about fixing bust-up, broken-down bodies – and it's *you* doing the fixing!

BODY BREAKDOWNS AND RECOVERY

Your human body is designed to last a lifetime, but as Dr Grimgrave is sure to remind us, "what can go wrong, will go wrong". Sometimes your body's self-repair systems need a helping hand and these unique trouble-shooting charts explain what YOU, the body owner, can do, and what needs expert attention. They come complete with Dr Grimgrave's advice on common body problems – THANKS DOC!

TROUBLE-SHOOTING CHART 1: THE HEAD

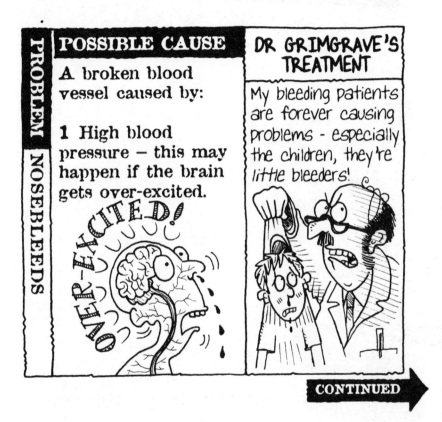

PROBLEM NOSEBLEEDS

POSSIBLE CAUSE

A broken blood vessel caused by:

1 High blood pressure – this may happen if the brain gets over-excited.

OVER-EXCITED!

DR GRIMGRAVE'S TREATMENT

My bleeding patients are forever causing problems - especially the children, they're *little* bleeders!

CONTINUED ➡

2 Dry air damaging the wall of the nose's blood vessels.

3 Explosive nose blowing or nasty nose-picking by body owners.

BLAST!

PICK!

Pinch their nostrils and lean them forward for a few minutes.

They shouldn't blow the nose for a couple of days or they'll blow their chances of healing.

Flaking of head skin cells due to an infection by microbes.

Use an anti-dandruff shampoo.

DRUFF STUFF

An idiot once asked me how you catch dandruff. "In a paper bag!" I replied.

TROUBLE-SHOOTING CHART 2: THE DIGESTIVE SYSTEM

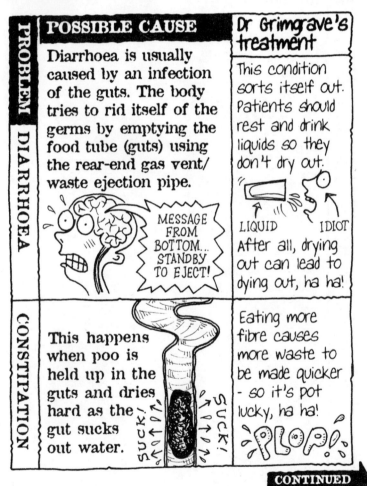

PROBLEM	POSSIBLE CAUSE	Dr Grimgrave's treatment
DIARRHOEA	Diarrhoea is usually caused by an infection of the guts. The body tries to rid itself of the germs by emptying the food tube (guts) using the rear-end gas vent/ waste ejection pipe. MESSAGE FROM BOTTOM... STANDBY TO EJECT!	This condition sorts itself out. Patients should rest and drink liquids so they don't dry out. LIQUID IDIOT After all, drying out can lead to dying out, ha ha!
CONSTIPATION	This happens when poo is held up in the guts and dries hard as the gut sucks out water. SUCK! SUCK!	Eating more fibre causes more waste to be made quicker - so it's pot lucky, ha ha! PLOP!

CONTINUED →

It can be caused by lack of roughage, which slows food and poo down as it moves through the guts.

(HE'S SITTING ON THE LOO)

BRAN FLAKES (ROUGHAGE)

URGH!

Laxatives make the patient produce waste, but I keep my surgery toilet locked. When the laxatives work it's amusing to watch the patients make a fast exit!

LOO

Vomiting happens when the stomach ejects its contents. This may have many causes. Fear, gut infections and foul food can all produce this revolting result.

VOMIT!

Patients need to consume a sweet drink in small sips to avoid drying out.

SIP!

Of course, vomit can be fascinating to study - see my case notes. I always keep a jar or two of vomit to study over dinner!

Curious case study: It's tough on the throne

King Ferdinand I of Naples (1751–1825) had chronic constipation. When the straining sovereign found the going tough, he invited a crowd of friends into the royal toilet to keep him company. The Austrian Emperor Joseph (1741–1790) was one of them:

WE MADE CONVERSATION FOR MORE THAN HALF AN HOUR AND I BELIEVE HE WOULD STILL BE THERE IF A TERRIBLE STINK HAD NOT CONVINCED US THAT ALL WAS OVER.

BAFFLING BODY CHANGES

Eventually, young human bodies start to change in a strange fashion. Now, this isn't really a body breakdown, but it sometimes feels like one to the bewildered body owner. The body may sprout hair in unusual places. (This isn't new hair because human bodies have more hair than chimps, remember? But each hair is longer and thicker than before.)

Anyway, do you know what that means? No, silly, they're not turning into werewolves! It's worse than that – they're turning into *teenagers!*

Dear reader, I have a puzzling problem. The Monster is acting in a freakish fashion. He is becoming horribly hairy. He even has three wispy hairs on his chin that he proudly shaves each day. His muscles are getting bigger. He's friendly with those brainless young zombies, and he's taking an unusually close personal interest in the Vampire. What in the name of horror is happening?

BODY DATA

1 There is no need for you, the body owner, to be bothered by blushing. It's perfectly normal and happens when your brain runs a feeling-embarrassed program. Your brain squirts a chemical into your blood. It makes blood vessels widen under your skin and turns fair skin red.

2 A teenager's voice sounds deeper because the vocal cords that make the sounds of the voice are getting bigger. Large male bodies have bigger vocal cords, so they make deep, gruff, growling sounds.

Becoming a teenager is a pre-programmed body body-changing phase designed to take several years. What happens depends on what body type you own – girls turn into women, boys turn into men. Girls often start to change about two years before boys. At this point girls may become taller than boys – but the boys catch up.

Meanwhile, a girl's ovaries and a boy's testes squirt chemicals called hormones into their blood. (*Hey, who says teenagers are lazy?*) A boy's hormones make bigger muscles and his body appears more hairy. Hormones make a girl's body have periods, grow hair in private regions and become more curvy.

BODY DATA

A little hormone goes a long way. Imagine a swimming pool filled with blood. (Yes, I know it would look gross and you wouldn't want to learn to swim in it but stick with me.) One little pinch of salt added to all that blood equals the proportion of hormones in a teenager's body.

Now, let's look at some teenage body problems…

TROUBLE-SHOOTING CHART 3: COMMON PROBLEMS IN TEENAGE BODY MODELS

PROBLEM	POSSIBLE CAUSE	DR GRIMGRAVE'S TREATMENT
BODY STINKS	Teenage and adult bodies ooze oily sweat around the armpits and rude bits. Munching microbes feed on the gungy grease and make sickening smells.	Regular clean clothes and a good wash with germ-killing soap.

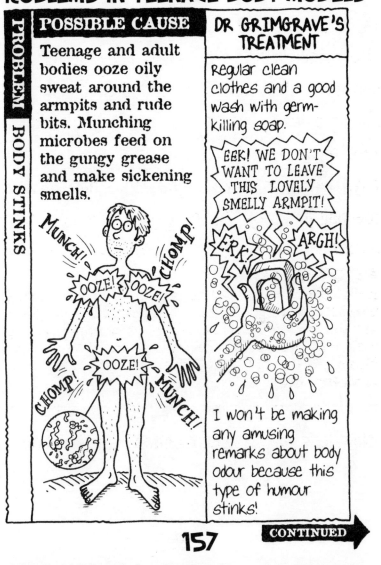

EEK! WE DON'T WANT TO LEAVE THIS LOVELY SMELLY ARMPIT!

ERK!

ARGH!

MUNCH!

CHOMP!

OOZE! OOZE!

OOZE!

CHOMP!

MUNCH!

I won't be making any amusing remarks about body odour because this type of humour stinks!

CONTINUED ➤

EEK!

Caused by germs. It's made worse by a dry mouth (not drinking enough water), failure of the body owner to clean their teeth, smoking or drinking alcohol or eating onions or garlic. Pfwoar!

The patient should use mouthwash and clean their teeth - or suffer a nasty "brush" with their dentist.

If a patient has bad breath *and* smelly feet, it's probably foot and mouth disease, ha ha!

BODY LANGUAGE

A body expert says…

Do you say…

I STUDY HALITOSIS (HALLY-TOE-SIS).

YOU LOOK AT HAYLEY'S TOES — YUCK! WHO IS HAYLEY ANYWAY?

No, it's worse than that! The body expert studies bad breath – halitosis is the posh body expert's jargon for a manky mouth.

BODY DATA

1 Any body can suffer from bad breath – but it's especially terrifying for teenagers when they meet their boy or girlfriends. Did you know the human body spends a total of two weeks in lip-puckering, soppy-sloppy snogging or kissing? Body experts think this is a good work-out of the face muscles.

2 Some body owners tried traditional smelly feet treatments. One method involved stuffing your socks with bran to soak up sweat. It didn't work but you could invent stinky cheesy-bran breakfast cereal...

Curious case study: A low-down dirty crook

In 2,000, a robber held up a bank in San Diego, USA. It seems everyone held their noses rather than sticking their hands up because the man was so smelly! Hmm, he sounds more like a "rank" robber! Police helicopters blared loudspeaker warnings about the smelly man. Soon afterwards, a nosy motel receptionist noticed a nasty niff from a new guest. She called the cops. A good detective follows his nose and that's just what the cops did – the man was soon arrested and "scent" to jail. He should have taken a bath – he'd have made a clean getaway!

SPOTS, BOILS AND ZITS

The Monster is excited because the Vampire has invited him to her tomb. But this morning a terrible scream rang from the bathroom. The Monster has pimples, or zits as young persons call them! His face looks like a dot-to-dot puzzle!

I told the Monster that 80% of teenagers suffer spots. They are caused by the body over-producing oily fluids to protect the skin. This is caused by hormones. The spots form  as the skin's oil tubes are blocked and infected by gruesome germs. I fear the Monster was not paying attention. He was moaning in panic and trying to squeeze his pimples. AARGH! That spurt of pus hit my eyeball!

That young idiot is making his spots worse! If germs from his fingers get into the spot it will become even more infected. He should wash the oil off his hair and skin each day and use an anti-spot fluid and cleansing pads. Meanwhile, if the young fool wants to go on a "date", as young persons call it, he should wear a paper bag over his head. Pleasure's too good for the young, you know.

GRIMGRAVE
1942

WORRISOME WARTS...

And talking about skin problems, warts have attracted more than their fair share of freaky folk remedies. Oh no – the Baron's got that book again. And if I don't show you he'll be doing experiments on my eyeballs!

BARON FRANKENSTEIN'S SECRET BOOK OF CURES

REMEDIES FOR WARTS

I am of the opinion that a few warts improve a face but as usual everyone else disagrees! That's why I am plotting to try these traditional treatments on the Monster if he ever gets warts...

IS THAT THE BEST YE CAN DO?

THE DOG'S PEE TREATMENT ~ The pee was smeared on the warts. This was a popular Tudor treatment – well, I don't think it was popular with anyone with warts, ha ha! If this didn't work, the sufferer could always try rubbing the warts with pig's blood oinkment, er, ointment

THE DEAD SLUG ~ Get a fat slimy slug from the garden and crush it and smear the

THIS SHOULD DO THE TRICK!

mashed-up slug-juice all over the warts. If this doesn't work you could catch a grasshopper and make it gnaw the warts with its strong jaws.

THE CAT'S TAIL TREATMENT

You need to stroke the warts with a tortoiseshell cat's tail during the month of May. Hmm, I wonder where I can find such a cat? Do I have to cut its tail off?

NO! YOU DON'T!

THE DRIBBLE TREATMENT ~ You dribble over the warts first thing in the morning. I am told that in Kansas, USA in the 1990s,

WARTS WRONG WITH YOU LOT?

children who suffered from warts were taken to church. After prayers, a woman known as "the wart lady" licked the children's warts with the tip of her tongue. Hmm, even I think that sounds cruel!

I wonder if any of these treatments work? Obviously not, judging by Dr Grimgrave's reaction…

BAH HUMBUG! BALDERDASH! CODSWALLOP!

ACHING ADULT BODY MODELS

If you own a smaller body you'll be used to adult body owners giving you body care advice. Much of this advice is sound and sensible but it should be pointed out that some adult body owners don't look after their own bodies too well. Fuelling the body on too much alcohol, tobacco and drugs causes MAJOR body problems. Who says that adult body owners are *always* right?

Read this next bit or regret it later…

DANGEROUS DRINKING, SMOKING AND DRUGS

1 Alarming alcohol: The human body doesn't need alcohol and doesn't want alcohol – even if the body owner is gagging for it! Alcohol soaks into the blood via the stomach and then the liver has to remove 28 grams of alcohol every hour. This means the body can drink a small glass of beer in one hour and not get drunk. Any more alcohol escapes into the blood and affects the brain for a few hours.

Now, my dear readers, I would like to tell you the story of how alcohol affected the Monster at the Zombie's Halloween Party...

Midnight: Monster's first drink. At this stage the Monster looks fairly normal... well, normal by his standards, ha ha!

12.30: Monster's third drink.

Alcohol dries the germ-killing spit and causes smelly breath.

Red face as alcohol widens blood vessels under the skin.

1 a.m.: Monster's fourth drink.

I ROAM GRAVEYARDS, I DIG UP BODIES, I SCARE VICARS... IT'S A REAL SCREAM...

YAWN!

Alcohol weakens hearing — making the Monster talk louder. The befuddled Monster thinks he's being funny when he's actually being boring.

2 a.m.: Monster's sixth drink.

I GESH THESH NO RESHT FOR THE WICK -HIC -KED...

Alcohol confuses the brain's speech systems.

Clumsy actions due to alcohol affecting the brain's movement controls.

Wider blood vessels mean more blood goes to the kidneys. The kidneys make more pee.

ER – S'CUSE ME!

Alcohol upsets the stomach causing vomiting.

165

I WANT TO DIE!

YOU'LL HAVE TO COME ALIVE FIRST!

Alcohol dries out the body causing headache, tiredness and sickness. This stage is known as the hangover.

An idiot thought my surgery was a pub and said he felt like a bottle of wine, so I told him to put a cork in it, ha ha! In fact, one or two alcoholic drinks aren't harmful - I've been known to indulge in the odd glass of wine after a hard day dealing with idiots. Small amounts of alcohol may reduce the danger of blood clots in blood vessels.

2 Terrible tobacco: Some body owners reckon that smoking is cool and grown-up and daring. OK, so why don't they jump off a cliff? It's definitely daring and it could prove less risky than smoking. Take a close look at what's in these cigarettes…

Yes, you spotted it. ALL THESE SUBSTANCES ARE POISONOUS. That's right, they all harm the body! Like most doctors, Dr Grimgrave holds firm anti-smoking views…

Anyone who smokes should be allowed to smoke as much as they like - just so long as they're on top of a bonfire, ha ha! One of my idiot patients, Mrs Ashtray, smokes and is overweight. Yes, she's a heavy smoker. This woman is a school dinner lady. She smokes in the kitchen and flicks her disgusting ash into the boiled cabbage and custard. This causes the children to vomit over their teachers, and the head-teacher isn't brave enough to tell her off.

PATIENT RECORD: STRICTLY CONFIDENTIAL

NAME: Mrs Ashtray

DIAGNOSIS: Mrs Ashtray suffers from smoking. The effects are obvious:

Wrinkled skin caused by tobacco poisons killing cells. Brown teeth (tobacco stains). Loss of teeth caused by gum disease.

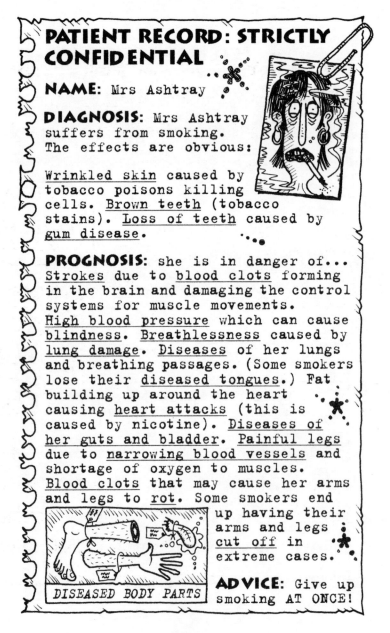

PROGNOSIS: she is in danger of... Strokes due to blood clots forming in the brain and damaging the control systems for muscle movements. High blood pressure which can cause blindness. Breathlessness caused by lung damage. Diseases of her lungs and breathing passages. (Some smokers lose their diseased tongues.) Fat building up around the heart causing heart attacks (this is caused by nicotine). Diseases of her guts and bladder. Painful legs due to narrowing blood vessels and shortage of oxygen to muscles. Blood clots that may cause her arms and legs to rot. Some smokers end up having their arms and legs cut off in extreme cases.

DISEASED BODY PARTS

ADVICE: Give up smoking AT ONCE!

168

I ought to point out that these are just the NICER effects of smoking. Doctors believe that every cigarette shortens the life of a human body by five minutes.

Mrs A won't give up smoking because her body is gasping for nicotine. Cigarettes switch her brain to calm but alert mode. Going without nicotine is tough and that's why most smokers would carry on smoking even if they had to smoke banknotes. What a pity! The sooner a smoker gives up, the better their health is going to be.

So Dr Grimgrave has decided to be cruel to be kind. He's had a word with the Baron. And the Baron (who is kind of cruel too) has agreed to take away Mrs Ashtray's cigarettes and lock her in his dungeon until she agrees to give up smoking *for ever*…

3 Dangerous drugs

AN IMPORTANT MESSAGE TO BODY OWNERS…

There are a lot of dangerous drugs around, but body owners only need to know *three* things about them…

• All banned drugs are poisonous in large amounts.

• The trade in banned drugs is controlled by cold-hearted criminals who aren't nice people to give money to. Why not pay to help fluffy little kittens and playful puppies? They're far more deserving!

• No one has ever found lasting happiness by taking drugs. Many have found lasting unhappiness and some have found even more long-lasting death.

WHINGEING WRINKLIES

As time goes by, owners of older bodies grumble more and more about their body's faults and problems. It's a sure sign that their bodies are beginning to wear out. Body experts call this process ageing and it's horribly complicated – but Dr Grimgrave's latest book explains everything...

CHAPTER 14
AGEING

IT'S ONLY A MATTER OF TIME, YOU KNOW

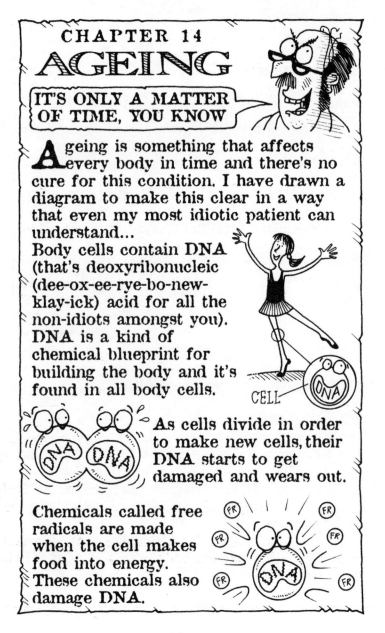

Ageing is something that affects every body in time and there's no cure for this condition. I have drawn a diagram to make this clear in a way that even my most idiotic patient can understand...

Body cells contain DNA (that's deoxyribonucleic (dee-ox-ee-rye-bo-new-klay-ick) acid for all the non-idiots amongst you). DNA is a kind of chemical blueprint for building the body and it's found in all body cells.

CELL

As cells divide in order to make new cells, their DNA starts to get damaged and wears out.

Chemicals called free radicals are made when the cell makes food into energy. These chemicals also damage DNA.

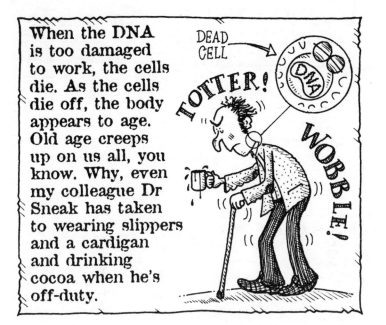

When the DNA is too damaged to work, the cells die. As the cells die off, the body appears to age. Old age creeps up on us all, you know. Why, even my colleague Dr Sneak has taken to wearing slippers and a cardigan and drinking cocoa when he's off-duty.

DEAD CELL

DNA

TOTTER!

WOBBLE!

BODY DATA

Yes, I know that DNA damage from making energy is a major design fault, but this shouldn't stop you feeding your body in order to keep it working. Hey – wait a moment! Trust Dr G to leave out the good news! Body owners can't stop their bodies ageing, but they can slow ageing down!

1 Taking lots of exercise slows the loss of muscle cells. This will keep your body in good condition in its later years.

2 Choosing the right food also helps. Chemicals called antioxidants soak up nasty free radicals and defend your body's DNA. These crucial chemicals include vitamin C in fresh fruit and vegetables and vitamin E in wholemeal bread and brown rice.

So, body owners, it helps to be keen on greens and nice about rice.

A MESSAGE TO ADULT BODY OWNERS...

Adult body owners will be thrilled to hear that red wine contains antioxidants! I bet some body owners will be so keen to get the health benefits that they'll open a few extra bottles to make sure they're getting enough! Don't forget the problems of drinking too much alcohol (see page 164).

And now let's look at some of the problems that bodies encounter as a result of ageing. Can Dr Grimgrave offer any hope of putting them right? Thought not…

TROUBLE-SHOOTING CHART 4: OLDER BODY TYPES

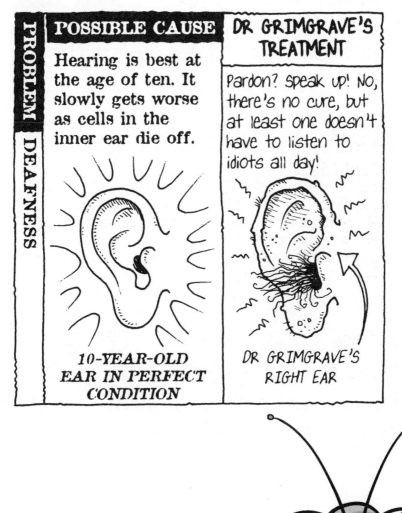

PROBLEM

DEAFNESS

POSSIBLE CAUSE

Hearing is best at the age of ten. It slowly gets worse as cells in the inner ear die off.

10-YEAR-OLD EAR IN PERFECT CONDITION

DR GRIMGRAVE'S TREATMENT

Pardon? speak up! No, there's no cure, but at least one doesn't have to listen to idiots all day!

DR GRIMGRAVE'S RIGHT EAR

PROBLEM		
BALDNESS	All bodies lose hair as they age as a result of cells dying off. But balding in males (like noses) can run in families.	There is no cure for this condition so don't waste my time. GRRR! [2]
DRY MOUTH	Older people make less spit due to a loss of cells in the spit production units in the mouth.	Lack of germ-killing spit results in more mouth microbes and bad breath and wind. The wind has the same cause as wind due to fast eating on page 109. Patients with this problem are ordered to wait outside!

1962   1982   2002

THOSE WERE THE DAYS!

---

2 By the way I should have warned you that Dr Grimgrave is a bit touchy about his own baldness.

High energy ultraviolet rays in sunlight kill skin cells that make collagen. This makes skin sag and wrinkle.

It helps to avoid being in the sun too long. A suntan isn't too appealing when it's a-peeling, ha ha. A good sunblock is required for all idiots who spend any time in the sun. That way they won't waste my valuable time!

BODY LANGUAGE

Dr Grimgrave says…

I SUFFER FROM ALOPECIA (AL-OH-PEE-SHA)

Do you say…

IS THAT WHY YOU'RE WEARING A STUPID HAT?

Correct! It's what body experts call balding. Oh well, it's hair today, gone tomorrow. Oh dear, I don't think Dr G appreciates my little joke. But the body *does* provide a kind of consolation prize. Hair begins to sprout from the eyebrows and nostrils and ears – isn't that nice? Did you know that some men grow two metres of nostril hair in a lifetime? It's lucky the hairs fall out otherwise men would trip over them. Now where did we put that electric nostril-hair plucker?

Curious case study: Bald, bad and brutal

Tsar Paul (1754–1801), Emperor of Russia, was the none-too-proud owner of a bald-bonced body. This was a seriously sensitive subject. One day a stupid soldier pointed at the sovereign's slap-head saying, "Look, there's baldy." The cruel Tsar heard the comment and ordered his guards to flog the soldier to death (I bet the poor man bald, I mean bawled, really loudly).

Next, power-crazed Paul banned the word "bald" from dictionaries and announced that anyone who dared to say the word would be executed.

You'll be pleased to hear that the ruthless ruler was killed by his soldiers and today Russians can use the B-word without fear of death.

BODY OWNER'S BALDNESS-CURE QUIZ

For many years the owners of balding bodies have seen the loss of head hair as a major design fault and have tried to put it right. Our fearless Horrible Science artist volunteered to try the Baron's traditional treatments.

BEFORE — 'TRIFFIC! I CAN'T WAIT!'

AFTER — GRRR!

Sorry, Tony! Anyway, all you have to do is match each substance to the treatments below...

Substance used:
1 Horse pee.
2 Cowpat.
3 A dead rat.
4 Green tea, honey and monkey bladders.

Treatment:
a) Drink it.
b) Eat it.
c) Put it on the scalp.

A NOTE TO YOUNGER BODY OWNERS...

It can be a challenge to work out how old a human body is... Take your teacher, for example – even if you dare ask, you're sure to suffer an unspeakable teacher torture. Well, here's how you can work out if a body really is ancient – or whether it's still quite young but it's had a hard life ...

TEST YOUR BODY 6: HOW ANCIENT IS YOUR TEACHER?

You will need:
• A younger body
• An ancient body (It helps if your

two bodies are related — but if
they're not, that's OK. Any old body
will do.)

What you do:
1 Compare the length of their ear lobes.

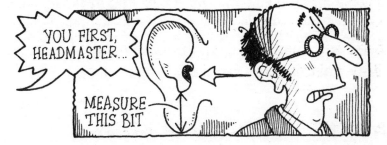

2 Compare the length of their teeth.

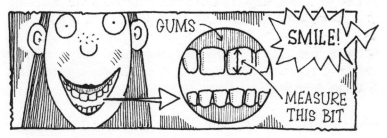

You should find:
1 Older bodies often have saggy ear
lobes. They get longer during the
body's life and the force of gravity
pulls them downward.

2 The old saying is right — older bodies really are "long in the tooth"! Ageing makes the gums shrink and the teeth appear longer.

A MESSAGE FROM THE AUTHOR

Vintage bodies should never be written off. Many of the problems described above are quite minor faults and a well-cared-for body of advanced years is still capable of many years of useful service.

Well, that's lucky because there's plenty of work for an old body. Jobs like looking after brand-new bodies. And by some eye-popping coincidence, that's what the next chapter is all about. Brand-new bodies and all their crazy care needs — but be warned! These beastly little bodies aren't quite potty-trained! Read on at your own risk!

BRAND-NEW BODIES

Human bodies do more than walk and talk and pee and poo and sleep and dream. They're also designed to produce *more* human bodies. Just think about it! You may own a TV, but I bet it can't turn into *two* TVs! And that automatic bum-scratcher isn't going to make you a new one in a million billion years. But human bodies are actually *designed* to make brand-new human bodies, or babies as they're commonly known!

Of course, this is very technical and advanced stuff for body owners, but fortunately we have our experts to guide us. The Baron has just built a baby out of body bits. He's calling her "Little Monster". Here she is now with her proud creator...

LITTLE MONSTER, STOP SUCKING THAT THUMB AND PUT IT BACK IN THE JAR WITH THE OTHER BODY BITS...

SUCK! SUCK!

Of course, you should NEVER try to build a baby from spare body bits. As I said, your body is programmed to do the job automatically

HOW THE BODY MAKES A BABY

The first thing that happens is that a human body pairs up with another human body. Two adult human bodies are needed (one male and one female – they're often described as parents). It helps if the bodies in question are:

a) Alive.

b) In love with one another.

At this point the body owners ask themselves if they're willing to feed the new body and love it and look after it in the years before the brand-new human body (baby) is able to look after itself.

The two adult bodies are fully equipped to make the baby. The female (known as the mother) produces a tiny DNA-containing micro-production unit – an egg. The egg comes from one of two high-tech assembly and storage units called ovaries. The male (often referred to as the father) makes millions of smaller micro-engineered DNA-delivery units, known as sperm, in his testes. Each sperm is designed to carry a copy of the male's DNA to the egg.

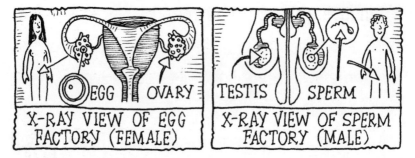

X-RAY VIEW OF EGG FACTORY (FEMALE)

X-RAY VIEW OF SPERM FACTORY (MALE)

Body owners can let their bodies get down to the mingling of sperm and egg with (hopefully) lots of fun and romance and love sensations running in their sensory equipment. But, since 1978, it's also been possible for scientists to do the necessary mixing in a less romantic test tube.

THE INCREDIBLE EGG AND SPERM RACE

Body owners are sure to be interested in what happens inside the female's body once the sperm gets there. Basically, the sperm do what they're designed to do: swim to the egg. For the sperm, it's a tough long-distance marathon. It's like a full-sized body swimming 11 km – that's 1,375 lengths of a large swimming pool. Let's see how this one's getting on…

Our sperm beats its little tail and races about 70 million other sperm. It's hard work – it takes 1,000 tail beats to get 1 cm and there are dangerous white blood cells to dodge on the way. Hey, keep going little guy!

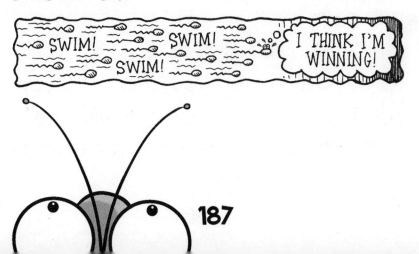

BODY DATA

Allowing for the size difference, the human body can't swim as fast as a microscopic sperm. A strong swimmer can manage 11 km per hour, but some sperm race the equivalent distance in a few minutes. Only about 100 sperm make it to the egg. But 69,999,900 don't – they die. The surviving sperm squirt chemicals that dissolve the egg's protective wall. The egg is about 1,000 times bigger than them – so it's a bit like alien tadpoles burrowing into a big squidgy asteroid. But, at last, our sperm triumphantly dives inside.

It's so excited, bless it, that its little tail falls off. Now it's time for the vital body-planning session. Over the next few hours the entire appearance of a new human body is hammered out. What's happening is that the sperm and egg combine their DNA to make a blueprint for the new human being. Let's hope they agree on the details!

BODY DATA

German body expert Paracelsus (1493–1541) claimed you could make a body without a soul by mixing sperm and horse dung for 40 days. Hmm, this would explain sinister scientists, dangerous dinner ladies and terrible teachers. Well, it would if it had worked.

All you body owners reading this might well think that making a new body sounds horribly complicated – and you'd be right! But in fact we've only reached the *start* of a nine-month process. This ends only when the new body is released from its development capsule in the female – this is known as being born.

FIVE FACTS THAT NOT TOO MANY BODY OWNERS KNOW ABOUT MAKING BABIES

1 The egg roots itself in the mother's womb, or uterus as body experts call it. As the baby develops it gets fed through a feeding tube linked to a life-support system called the placenta.

2 In its first month, the baby's cells are dividing every two days. It doesn't sound a lot but if your body grew this fast at the age of nine, you would be the size of Mount Everest in just thirteen days.

3 Unborn babies float in a bubble of fluid. They pee in their fluid and then drink it. They also wave their arms, perform somersaults and open and shut their mouths. I guess they're just showing off.

4 Two babies being made at the same time are called twins. Twins often fight before they're born. Then they kiss and hold one another. Oh isn't that sweet?

5 By week 19 the baby is covered in hair. The hair drops out by week 26 – if it didn't babies would be born with beards and hairy legs.

BODY LANGUAGE

Dr Grimgrave says:

Do you say...

YOU'VE GOT AN UMBILICUS

WHO'S UNCLE LUCUS?

PROD!

ANSWER

NO! The umbilicus is yet another bit of posh body expert's jargon. This word means the hole where the feeding tube joined your body – you might call it a belly button.

Being born is tough for the baby. As soon as it emerges from its mother it's got seconds to rearrange the blood flow around its heart and fill its lungs' air inlet/exhaust system with air and not water. If it doesn't manage this it suffers a total body breakdown. Thankfully, nearly every baby makes it. And there it is – a brand-new human body in full working order!

The baby's first view of the world is deeply scary. Apart from the shock of seeing its parents for the first time (that must be *really* scary!) it can't see properly. A baby's brain can't handle vision yet and it sees double – that's *two* sets of parents – both upside down! No wonder newborn babies cry!

BODY DATA
New babies produce green poo. They haven't pooed for nine months and the green colour comes from a build-up of bile digestive juice made by the liver. Older body owners should make sure their bodies eject waste more often than this. And now let's see what Dr Grimgrave has to say about babies...

In my honest opinion ALL newborn babies are plug-ugly. Here's a typical strange-looking case...

Often their heads are squashed as they are born. The bones in a baby's skull haven't yet fused together. (This is quite harmless and later puts itself right.)

Blotchy skin, wrinkles, and puffy red eyes.

One-quarter of a baby's body length is head and a baby's head is as wide as its shoulders.

If one of my idiot patients looked like that the other patients would scream and run a mile, leaving me with a nice empty waiting room. That'll be the day - sigh! But doting (dotty) parents have a totally different reaction...

DOTING, DOTTY PARENTS

BODY DATA

According to body experts, every human brain (except Dr Grimgrave's) is programmed to find baby faces cute and appealing. The brain also runs stress programmes when it hears a baby crying. This is about to happen to the Baron's brain ...

WAAAAAH!

OK, SO YOU DON'T WANT TO PLAY WITH THE EYEBALLS - WELL WHAT IS WRONG, MY LITTLE MONSTER-KINS?

I find all this silliness and nonsense deeply depressing. It will all end in tears of course - usually baby tears. Babies cry when they want things - usually a cuddle or to belch or break wind (or fart as some rude persons say). Most often it's because they want a feed, the ill-mannered little brats...

In fact, adult female bodies are equipped with a built-in portable refuelling system for hungry babies. It's so good it sells itself...

At this stage in the chapter, body owners might be wondering what use babies really are. After all, what do they actually do? Eat, sleep, burp, poo, pee? Wrong! Baby bodies are programmed by their DNA to develop and change 24 hours a day – and NOTHING is going to get in their way…

For example, at birth the new human body is just one-twentieth of the weight of a full-sized human body, but its weight is designed to increase *four* times in two years. In two years, the baby body will have crawled 150 km and self-programmed its brain with the correct data and balance control to allow itself to walk.

Actually, walking is harder than it looks because it involves learning how to use 200 muscles in the right order, but brilliant babies take it all in their stride and they go on to do something no animal in history has ever managed … they talk!

BODY DATA

1 In the 1970s scientist Herbert Terrace tried to teach a baby chimp named Nim to use sign language. Like a human baby, Nim learnt to be naughty and use a potty, but he only learnt 125 word signs in four years. Human baby brains store over 1,500 words in the same period. So poor Nim proved to be more of a chimp than a champ.

SIGN LANGUAGE FOR, "WELL, WHAT D'YOU EXPECT? I'M ONLY A CHIMP, YOU IDIOT!"

2 And the human brain goes on to store thousands more words. Well, that's handy because your body chatters on for a lifetime total of ten years. Now that really is something to talk about! And of course knowing lots of words and what they look like on a page has helped your body to read this book for you.

Well, body owners, your *Body Owner's Handbook* is almost over. We just have time for the final chapter – now where did I leave it? What's that, Little Monster? You did WHAT on it?

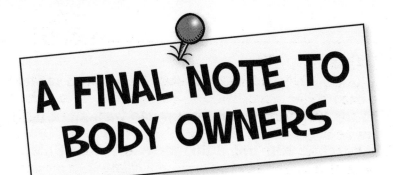

A FINAL NOTE TO BODY OWNERS

As you've just found out, being a body owner is a full-time job. Despite its incredible automatic features, your body really does depend on you to work properly. In fact, that's what this whole handbook has been about, making friends with your body!

Making friends with your body means looking after it properly. It means giving it the right fuel and an exercise routine that boosts its performance in years to come. You'll see the most benefit if your body is new and growing. But even a battered old banger of a body can be improved by a bit of tender loving care and the right bodywork treatment, so here's your ultimate…

BODY OWNER'S HANDBOOK ADVICE

• Give your body plenty of exercise to build the powerful muscles and lungs and heart that will keep your body going strong for a long lifetime. And regular exercise helps to postpone ageing in full-sized bodies.

• The more your brain practises a skill, the better it gets. The more work your brain does, the faster and smarter it gets.

• Giving your body the right food builds a strong body that lasts even longer. This means fuelling it on a range of fresh food and lots of fruit and vegetables with those amazing antioxidant goodies.

No body comes with a guarantee but a cared-for body certainly lasts longer. And that's a good thing because your body – like every other human body – is incredible. OK, so it can't run like cheetah, swim like a seal or hear like a bat. But your body can do millions of jobs that no animal can ever do. And its power is limited only by the imagination program in your amazing brain! So enjoy your body. After all, it's the only body you'll ever get and it's all yours – for life!

HORRIBLE INDEX